Purposeful Living

Building an Authentic Life and Legacy

Ella Coleman

EllaVation Publishing
P.O. Box 361895
Columbus, Ohio 43236

EllavationPublishing.com
www.EllaColeman.net
ellavatingu@live.com

Ordering information:
Special discounts are available on quantity purchases
by churches, businesses, organizations, and others.
For details, contact the publisher at the address above.

First Printing, 2014
Printed in the United States of America

DEDICATION

I dedicate this book to my special co-laborers who contributed to the production and publishing of *PURPOSE Magazine*. This work is a compilation of some of my writings and commentaries in *PURPOSE* during the tenure of these gifted and highly skilled people: Dr. Particia Wingard Carson, Gloria Hunter, Melanie Houston, Pamela C. Parker, Dr. Myles Munroe, Janelle Kinnard, Grace Hunter, Kojo Kamau, Larry Williamson, Ira Graham, III, Sandra Moody Gresham, Dr. Robert L. Lawson, Henry Ford, Lucius Lewis, Ilinda Reese, and Dr. Barbara Reynolds; and those who have passed on–Freddie L. Fulson, Willie Jennings, Mother Constance Johnson, Pamela Thornton, DeAntè Pierre Wilson, Sam Tyus, and Zig Ziglar. I so appreciate your love and support of the publishing portion of my vision.

ACKNOWLEDGMENTS

First, I thank God and my Lord and Savior Jesus Christ, for life, health, strength and inspiration, which I can do nothing without.

Second, I thank my gracious mother, Era, for providing me with a solid foundation of love, respect, and family values.

Also, I thank Apostles Eric and Carolyn Warren for their prayers and support.

A special thanks to Gloria Hunter for editing this book, Alleceia Walker for her skills and helpful input, and Robert Randolph for the front cover photo.

Table of Contents

INTRODUCTION

*P*urposeful Living is a compilation of inspirational writings aimed to encourage, equip, and challenge one to live purposefully. It is full of passionate and powerful messages permeated with principles and strategies for better living. More than 16 years of my selected editorial excerpts as publisher of *PURPOSE Magazine* are included in this work, as well as other freshly inspired renderings. These writings emphasize the importance of faith, purpose and vision while incorporating the Golden Rule–"Do unto others as you would have them do unto you."

The content of this book came by divine inspiration as I sought the Lord for wisdom applicable to modern daily living. Serious issues of today– the weakening of family, media's proliferation of sex and violence, the escalation of crime and scandals, etc.–are covered from a spiritual and biblical perspective. While personal and societal challenges are addressed, they are accompanied by workable solutions.

Purposeful Living is presented in five parts. Effectively relating to oneself through understanding identity, purpose, and vision is the focal point of part one. Part two deals with the dynamics of building healthy relationships. Part three expounds on how to appropriately handle change and transition. Part four covers securing stability through discipline and balance, while part five offers strategies for advancement through applying business principles of integrity.

An anthology such as this encompasses a range of subjects linked by a common thread tied to the heart of the author. Actually, the motive behind my message is simply: to help someone live a better and more meaningful life. So, the words herein were written with compassion.

The pages ahead resonate a cry from my heart for the discovery of truth, the experience of freedom, justice and peace, the reconciliation of broken relationships, and the healthy maturity of us all. I pray that the reading of this book inspires readers to go beyond routines, rituals, and norms to venture freely out of comfort zones for self-improvement, and to help others. It is in this free movement that we can obey God and carry out His dynamic, life-saving will on earth.

Ella Coleman

Part 1

Y O U

Personal Development

Chapter 1

AWAKENING THE AUTHENTIC YOU

Knowing or not knowing oneself impacts, for better or for worse, all other relationships and life experiences. Many husbands, wives, parents, children, siblings, relatives, and friends are not genuinely known for who they are, too often, because they don't know themselves. It is amazing that people can grow up, go to school, church, work together but still not genuinely know one another. At the heart of this dilemma is the fact that many are confused about their own true identity. The commentaries in this chapter address the identity issue while encouraging you to take action to awaken and express your authenticity.

The Power of Being Yourself

When who we are aligns with what we do, purpose is fulfilled. True identity and righteous actions combined produce powerful results. Anything short of living our true selves is not enough. As motivational speaker and author Henry Ford said, "Success is You." And truly, success without you is not success at all.

Being oneself is the most powerful of all expressions. Oprah Winfrey dared to just be herself on her talk show and became one of the most successful women in the television industry.

It would seem that being oneself–who God made you to be–would be fairly easy but it is not for many. The world system is set up to suppress our true identities through its mass classifications. We are classified by income levels, race, gender, education, etc. Of course, these are all part of our descriptions but do not determine who we really are.

The season has arrived for the genuine to override the superficial. The signs of the times declare it on the evening news. Through deceit, scandals, and conspiracy, truth cast down will always rise. The battles between good and evil that continue to rage externally in our natural environment, are

Being oneself is the most powerful of all expressions.

outward manifestations of inner conflicts in the souls and hearts of people. On a personal level, through all the commotion and distractions, it is still possible for one to discover true identity that supersedes labels and classifications.

The great humanitarian and caretaker, Mother Teresa, expressed herself, not caring what the world thought. As a result, the world had to bow to the agape love of God through which she impacted and transformed lives. Her funeral service was televised worldwide. This kind of victory and impact in life and death was a result of her pouring out herself in service to the disadvantaged, which was her purpose.

There are those who have mistakenly said, "Because I'm the 'wrong' color, I can't do this or that," when in fact, there is no "wrong color." The color with which we are born is the right color for each of us. This is what Dr. Martin Luther King, Jr. was trying to tell us. So, we don't have time to concentrate on skin color; it is a given. Because life is so short, our attention should be focused on more important matters like improving relationships, bettering health, helping the less fortunate, etc.

Those who have superior racist attitudes cannot be themselves. Therefore, they are not free to reach their potential. That old terrible destroyer–the spirit of the oppressor–is rooted inside the bigoted mindset

Courage is a major part of freedom and honest self-expression. Without confrontation, there is no freedom.

and emotions. So hatred must be completely kicked out of our lives in all the deceitful forms it manifests. Hatred says, "You're not good enough. Your hair, skin, lips or weight is not right; your family is not right. Transform yourself to be like "those people" and you'll be "professional and dignified." We must reply, "Get out hatred!"

Immediately, invite love in and think of the ways that you can creatively express it. Some do so through the arts. Others show love through caring for the sick and shut-in, while some release it through hugs and smiles. Jesus expressed love in its greatest form when He healed the sick, gave sight to the blind, speech to the mute, knowledge and wisdom to the ignorant; then gave his life freely for all people. He was able to do this because he knew himself and his purpose.

Courage is a major part of freedom and honest self-expression. Without confrontation, there is no freedom. Liberty usually require a fight or overcoming opposition. So the question is: are we willing to step out of the boundaries of comfort, complacency, and static tradition to do what may not be popular? Be liberated now from the opinions, suppression, and jealousies of others. Express the true you. Creatively declare your heart. Step out on that God-given vision or dream. Let's be true to ourselves even if it scares us. We can be who we are.

"For it was You who created my inward parts; You knit me together in my mother's womb... I have been remarkably and wonderfully made."
- Psalm 139:1-14 HCSB

Accurate Self-Assessment

Part of the preparation for moving ahead is being honest in our self-assessments. This means clearly evaluating the reasons for personal past experiences, as well as the reasons behind events, issues, crises, and other happenings in the world around us.

Order is one of the first laws of God's creation and it dictates that we must begin with ourselves, putting oneself in order before judging others.

> **Everything worthwhile begins at home and spreads abroad. Home is where the heart is.**

Meaningful changes begin in the heart, the home of desire, and spreads abroad. Deep desire manufactures motivation to act; to initiate improvements in our own thinking, deeds, and actions before looking to assess or judge other people or situations.

What has life been like for you and why? You may find it helpful to make a mental or written list of important occurrences in your life, both pleasant and unpleasant. (Remember, an unpleasant experience is not necessarily negative. Nor is a pleasant experience equivalent to being positive.) Look within, asking God to reveal the reasons for these experiences and the lessons you should learn, so you can move on to fulfill your greater purpose.

After we each deal with self, we can move on to the collective level of family, community, city, state, nation, and world. To operate effectively and responsibly in all that we have to reckon with outside of ourselves, we must advance from selfishness to selflessness. True service to God and fellow humans only comes when we make sacrifices of love, as did Jesus Christ, who made the ultimate sacrifice of his life for humanity.

"Understanding is a fountain of life to those who have it."
- Proverbs 16:22 KJV

Activating Potential

We must always consider our capabilities. How much of our potential are we using? Are we being the best that we can be, or are we settling for less? These questions should be asked on a regular basis.

The obvious answers can be packaged into one statement: There is always room for improvement. Improvement comes with an accurate and honest assessment of strong points, shortcomings and mistakes; the willingness to make a concentrated effort for positive change, along with patience and perseverance. But before we can travel the path of improvement, we must desire to improve.

Potential is an endowed capability that can be developed or actualized. Our potential can be realized and our purpose fulfilled when we apply our faith by stepping out into the area we have feared the most. Know that with God's help, we can be victorious.

There are many ways to activate potential. Perhaps starting a business, going back to school, letting go of meaningless, draining jobs and unhealthy relationships, or simply confronting a situation wisely that has been swept under the rug for too long. Sure, this kind of action is uncomfortable and challenging, but how bad do you want the change?

Desire is at the heart of any meaningful change we make in our lives. It is the motivating stimulus that moves us to action. Without desire, no one can pursue anything, particularly purpose. Les Brown, "The Motivator," says "We have to be HUNGRY!" And indeed we do; hungry to make our dreams come true, because in that deep urge to reach the goal, is the power to make it happen.

Pursuing and Discovering Purpose

The treasures of purpose are found in the chest of originality. It is the uniqueness in each of us that is most needed by others. Finding or creating a means through which that difference can be lovingly expressed is a critical pursuit. We should not allow anything or anyone to deter us from the path to actualization.

Divinely structured within the core of each person is a unique composition. Biologically, this substance causes a distinction in every human fingerprint. Spiritually, it stamps a purpose in the heart of each individual to be discovered and lived. When purpose has not been realized, frustration, confusion and a host of other negatives harbor in the soul.

As best-selling author, Dr. Myles Munroe, writes in his book, *In Pursuit of Purpose*, "When purpose is not known, abuse is inevitable." So, when we look around and see unhappiness and emptiness in talented and gifted people, it is because they do not know their purpose or they know it but are not living it.

> **The treasures of purpose are found in the chest of originality.**

Usually adversities and circumstances are a set-up and a part of the process to purpose and meaning. Recently, I watched an interview of the 1984 Olympic ski champion and paraplegic Bonnie St. John on "Life Today," hosted by James and Betty Robison. Interestingly, Bonnie, whose leg was amputated at age five, was sexually abused from age two to seven. Even with all of that weighing against her, her mother lovingly insisted on excellence and no excuses. She went on to become a ski champion, a wonderful mother, author and motivational speaker.

Bonnie shared her story to help others overcome insurmountable odds. She talked about how many times she fell and suffered trying to learn how to ski with one leg but noted the advantage she had over other skiers. Bonnie said she did not have to worry about her skis crossing because she only had one. Stories like this assure us that we can prevail and be triumphant even when we have a disadvantage.

"A setback is just a setup for a comeback," says award-winning motivational speaker and author, Willie Jolley. So many times what is considered a severely negative situation is really an opportunity waiting to be acted upon. But the outcome depends greatly on attitude and the decision of refusing to be defeated. If handled wisely, the problems we face provide the best clues to finding purpose and fulfillment.

"May He [God] grant you according to your heart's
desire and fulfill all your purpose." – Psalm 20:14 NKJV

Understanding the Purpose Process

The route to purpose is different for each individual. For one person, living purpose is as simple as making the choice to do what is in his or her heart. Still, for another, who is clueless of their reason for being, more is required. But one must, at least, be willing to pursue it.

Purpose must be brought to term before delivery. Being pregnant with purpose can be uncomfortable. The uneasiness, heaviness, and awkwardness may cramp your style but the life coming forth is well worth it. Note that purpose is dynamic and not stagnant, just as a fetus keeps moving in the womb and must turn to prepare for birth. Labor is not always easy and it can be painful. Yet, it is necessary to birth a vision.

Where are you in the process of God's purpose for your life? Perhaps you are already fulfilling it, but there is still more to accomplish. Or maybe you are frustrated because who you are does not line up with what you do. Do not fret. You are alive and can do something about it.

In reality, things are not always what they seem...that you'll never get there–to your rightful place–your unique identity and fitting function. Even though there seems to be a delay, you have the power to do your part. This means letting go of how you see things and focusing on the way God views things, which is recorded throughout the Bible. Talking about a shift, this requires major adjustments for most of us. Thoughts must also be reconfigured to accommodate the spiritual and intellectual potential coiled in your true identity.

Release the lion out of the lamb in you and walk into your greater purpose.

In some ways, who we are can be frightening. Just thinking about all the responsibility and work that comes with pursuing purpose or embarking upon a vision could cause one to run from it, ignore it, and perhaps, even deny it. But we are endowed with the power to conquer fear and intimidation, and abandon rejection. And as the battle rages, One much greater than us and the demons that haunts us, awaits our faithful action. Now, take courage. Release the lion out of the lamb in you and walk into your greater purpose.

"...Walk worthy of the calling with which you were called..." Ephesians 4:1b NKJV

Quiet Prayer Time

Being still and seeking the One who gave you your identity is the best way to realize true identity. To do so during these busy times, it must be made a priority.

Amidst our busy schedules, it is imperative, literally to book daily appointments with God. Our Creator knows all about who He intricately made each of us to be and why. Praying and sitting still with the Creator in quietness can calm, strengthen and focus the soul and spirit.

Quietness and prayer alter energy and body chemistry, causing molecules in the body to be less scattered and more centered. Then from deep within the heart, the core of us, the mystery of purpose is more likely to be revealed.

Consider, for some, a lifetime can be spent without taking the adequate introspective time so needed to gain clarity. Each of us has a specific reason for existing that is so precious, it warrants passionate pursuit.

Until it is recognized, life can seem routine, boring and even wasteful. It is in a meaningless maze that so many people merely exist. Loved ones and friends, Sunday morning sermons, motivational messages, and self-improvement books, although helpful, do not fill the void. It is critical to take quiet time each day to pray.

Chapter 2

BUILDING CHARACTER
ENHANCES IDENTITY

Virtues are priceless. The genuineness of a person with strong character and integrity is a blessing to cherish. Good character is usually the combination of innate and learned traits that have been tried, tested and refined over time. This chapter will provide applicable principles and wisdom for developing character complimentary to one's unique identity.

Shaping Character and Guarding It

Life is all about learning. Our very first breath thrusts us through a grand entrance into a world filled with sounds, images, feelings, and all types of stimuli. Even before birth, each baby's purpose has been established by the all-knowing, awesome God. The fertilization, formation and development of life are all provided so that each person may express his or her unique character and likeness with God.

Each impression made on an individual eases into the subconscious mind to merge with his or her true self–the human spirit. So, who each person is blends with the outside stimuli that have been absorbed. Just think, a gentle, sensitive, caring person impacted by a harsh and bitter environment could develop an off-balanced, cold and callous character. Or perhaps a stern, calculating, insensitive person influenced by a warm and loving family and surroundings could develop into an affectionate, sensitive character.

The same situations and circumstances impact all people differently, depending upon their perception and response. This tells us that being taught discretion and decision-making early is important. While proceeding through the various stages of life–infancy, childhood, adolescence, young adulthood, middle age, and the golden years–lesson after lesson and problem after problem is presented to test and build character. Less desirable experiences we are most resistant to, in most cases, are the ones that construct us into dynamic, resilient human beings.

> **Less desirable experiences we are most resistant to, in most cases, are the ones that construct us into dynamic, resilient human beings.**

Life's learning process is ongoing. On this plane, no one ever learns all. Our quest should be to learn as much as we can and to gain the wisdom to use that wealth of knowledge. To be well learned without wisdom is equivalent to being an educated fool. Moreover, no matter how much a foolish person learns, he or she never becomes truly wise. To be educated is to acquire an abundance of knowledge that may or may not be used wisely. An individual who obtains influential information or knowledge and does not know how to use it, is usually used by it.

In this age of information, many people are confused and disillusioned, especially young folks, because they have been bombarded with so much. It is no wonder the education system is failing so many children. These children are being assaulted by wicked computer and video games, music videos, X-rated movies, television, sex and violence, internet obscenity, and other unhealthy information. Parents, at least, should ban these subtle destroyers of character and life from their homes. All concerned should combat this spiritual, psychological, intellectual pollution by writing our congresspersons, the Federal Communications Commission, the President or Prime Minister, TV network decision-makers, as well as the creators of such profane products.

Also, we can counteract all this negative influence by creating and packaging positive information via billboards, signs, books, magazines, newspapers, blogs music, videos, websites, radio and television programs, video games, bumper stickers, and most of all, our own actions and life-styles. Like those who divisively promote misuse of their media to subtly deceive the masses for money, those who are dedicated to God–His morals and values–should use every possible medium to saturate the vast market with righteous messages.

> *"The heart of the wise teaches his mouth,*
> *and adds learning to his lips."* - Proverbs 16:23 NKJV

A Motive Check-Up

"What in the world are you doing?" is not only the title of a chal-lenging poem by author Clarressa Beckhon Thompson but an inquiry of accountability. The motives for what we do and why deserve serious exam-ination. Caught up in the rush of the day and era, time can easily slip away, leaving behind only a reality of how we spent it. Whether we use it wisely or foolishly, we reflect the sum total of every second, minute, hour, week, month, year, and decade of our lives.

In this vast garden called life, that which is planted and nurtured sprouts and grows–good, bad, or indifferent–bearing the fruits of our labor. Ultimately, we cannot camouflage the life we are living or the seeds we are

> **Ultimately, we cannot camouflage the life we are living or the seeds we are planting.**

planting.

Many of us are so busy but is it linked to our true purpose? Consider that a tremendous amount of energy and synergy are exerted daily into jobs, projects, programs, popular events, and lofty endeavors. But is fulfillment a fruit we enjoy as a result of our labor? Let's give ourselves what I call the "fulfillment of purpose test" as we personally answer the following ten questions.

1) Am I being myself?
2) Am I doing what is truly in my heart to do?
3) What are the motives of my current actions?
4) Are my thoughts, actions and work strictly for self or for the good of others as well?
5) Am I spending quality time with God, the children, family members, and friends He placed in my life?
6) Am I committed to a worthwhile cause?
7) Do I have short- and long-term goals for my life?
8) Am I working on a God-inspired vision, either my own or a corporate vision involving others?
9) Do I help someone other than myself each day?
10) Does my life set a good example for children and others to follow?

When these questions are honestly addressed and adhered to, then other questions that arise from numbing tragedies will not haunt us. Like international minister and author, Dr. Myles Munroe, I believe we were born to lead at some capacity but must be taught how. Good leadership starts with a healthy relationship with God and spreads to others.

As success advocate, Peter Lowe states, "Americans aren't sure you can be successful and love God. The Bible says you can't be successful without loving God." I must boldly declare, leadership that is not based in a love for God is dangerous. Why? Because God gives us life, breath, and all things (Genesis 2:7 and Acts 17:25); to have no love or reverence for God means spiritual blindness is present. If the blind leads the blind, both will fall into a ditch.

Love, responsibility and accountability are the checks and balances of good leadership. Oh, anyone can evade these three mandatory requirements, but it takes honesty, courage, commitment, and patience to embrace and live them. And when one is empowered with integrity and the aforementioned characteristics, his or her motive is pure.

"Live in peace with each other. And we urge you brothers, warn those who are idle, encourage the timid, help the weak, be patient with everyone."
- 1 Thessalonians 5:13-14 NIV

Problem-Solving Clues

As problems grip the world, know that with God, we have the ability to solve them. Most likely, the problem or issue that bothers you the most is probably where you were meant to serve or provide a solution. I recall watching a six-year-old little girl care for her sick aunt after school. Even though her aunt was terminally ill and had adult family caregivers and a professional nurse, her young niece assisted the nurse and would take care of her aunt when the nurse was not around.

That little girl grew up to become a nurse and has continuously been promoted because she gives excellent care to her patients and is preferred by the doctors with whom she works. In this case, we see that a natural response to a crisis or problem can set the stage for operating in one's calling or gift at a young age.

Complex situations arise to challenge and refine us. These issues are in our lives so we can rise to the occasion and do something about them, which many times have steered people directly or indirectly into their purpose or reason for being. Now, get excited about adversity and meet it with zeal, determination and a little laughter.

Opposition is one of the greatest influences of composition. Friction–the rubbing of two sticks together–ignites combustion. Fire purifies gold. Water, depending on the temperature to which it is exposed, can be boiled, vaporized or frozen. The crushing and fermentation of grapes produce wine. The connecting of negative and positive electrical wires illuminates a light bulb. Likewise, opposition builds and perfects character when handled wisely.

Meeting challenges enthusiastically opens our creative channels for the flow of workable solutions. This pushes us into the overcomers' realm of operation where quitting isn't an option; the place where goals are attained and vision is realized.

The people, places and things neglected are fertile ground for purpose discovery. Look around and see where there are needs not being met. Obviously, this does not require a great search. Perhaps meaning and fulfillment will take form when some of us dare to engage our assistance and problem-solving to serve others.

During my college years as a budding journalist, I interviewed a radio personality and community activist, the late Bill Moss, who said, "Ella, observe what is not being done and focus your attention on those overlooked, underserved areas." Those words stuck with me and I believe I heeded this advice when prompted by the Spirit to publish *Purpose Magazine*.

Although publishing was not necessarily in my initial plans for my life, it became an intricate part of my journey, predestined to happen. I saw a void in the media of positive, uplifting publications that was clear of alcohol and cigarette ads, seductive photos, and slanderous editorial content. So, I was moved to do something to counteract those destructive messages.

I know a lady who seemed to have attained desirable prosperity–God's blessings, a loving husband, children and family, a beautiful home, a good church home, wonderful friends, good health, and plenty of money. However, she shared with me one day over lunch that she was unhappy because as the mother of three small children, she had never been able to fulfill her dream of becoming an interior designer.

Since her children were then preteens, I suggested that she take some interior design courses and do some volunteer work in the field. When she did, her grades and work were so outstanding that she was able to land a position she really liked, on her on terms. Later, she started her own interior decorating company and became known for her excellent and unique work. When I saw her again, she exuded an enthusiasm she had not had prior to attaining her dream, which was a major part of her purpose.

Of all the things occurring in our world today, what bothers you the most? Before beginning a long list, there is one main factor that should be dealt with–self. How can one validly complain about the conditions of the world and the people in it, if he or she has not responsibly handled personal, family, and neighborhood problems?

"Consider Your Ways," a book by Eric L. Warren, provides biblical precepts, principles, and wisdom on character and integrity which address the root cause of most personal and world issues. Warren writes, "Character is the stamp or impression upon a person (or thing) that distinguishes it from any and all other persons or things. It is born out of a combination of ways of thinking and behaving, both of which are based upon a foundation of core virtues and/or vices. …Character is not a supplemental part of a person. Whether genetically, environmentally or spiritually induced, one's character is a manifestation of his/her inner nature." The type of character you have developed is an intricate part of your identity.

Perseverance and Rejuvenation

On the premises of honesty and integrity, step out on faith toward those special dreams and activate your heart's desire. Be willing to pay the price and go through the process because, ultimately, it's worth it. And it has been said, "What is worth having is worth fighting for." Press on, knowing that victory belongs to those who don't quit. Remember, over the hill of exhaustion, a second wind blows to revive a tired soul.

> **Remember, over the hill of exhaustion, a second wind blows to revive a tired soul.**

Surely, revival is a miracle experienced repeatedly throughout our lifetime. This resuscitating factor is an advantage that comes with being alive. Appreciate it, for it is like a well of living water to be drawn from when needed. But with revival comes responsibility to use that new energy to create and help others.

"The everlasting God, the Lord, the Creator of the ends of the earth, neither faints nor is weary. His understanding is unsearchable. He gives power to the weak, and to those who have no might, He increases strength. But those who wait on the Lord shall renew their strength; they shall mount up with wings like eagles, they shall run and not be weary, they shall walk and not faint."
- Isaiah 40:28, 29 & 31 NKJV

Chapter 3

CREATIVE POWER IN MOTION

H aving creativity means nothing if it is not used. So many people allow their creative gift to lie dormant and miss so many blessings. May your creativity be stirred while reading this chapter.

Creativity and Ideas

Endowed with creativity, we have the ability and responsibility to create. From the inkling of an idea, a spark of inspiration or the glimpse of a vision, emerge great manifestations of businesses, corporations, empires, ministries, books, inventions, recipes, fashion designs, etc. Such creative ideas are launched into motion by the application of faith and work, sustained through determination and perseverance, and matured with wisdom and patience. Therefore, it takes courage and discipline to develop and crystallize divinely inspired ideas that spring from the reservoir of purpose.

The application of one thought or one idea can transform one's life. So many people do not act upon their God-inspired ideas because of fear and intimidation. They are afraid of failing or losing what they have. But so much more is lost from clinging to complacency and settling for the false security of a job one hates for a paycheck of bondage. Creativity cannot flow freely in this type of stifling condition.

Creativity is a facilitator of purpose. Also, remember, wisdom should always be a part of every equation in life. Instead of abruptly quitting a job that meets your family's financial needs, carve out time to work on your idea or dream, during lunch breaks, in the evenings or on weekends. You must be determined.

Advancing Through and To Your Vision

Vision surpasses sight with vivid precision into the future, revealing in advance a magnificent outcome to work toward. But it's up to the visionary to transition that vision from idealism to realism. Vision is a beautiful futuristic view as it relates to your assignment or purpose in life. Vision, like desire, is a motivator of action that comes from the heart. It fuels passion and unveils purpose. Therefore, it is important to be steadfast in navigating the vision God gives you.

Vision is always bigger than the visionary, so realizing vision requires bold faith, determination and perseverance. Surely, it is more than a notion to conceive a vision and navigate it to full manifestation. It could very well happen in a short while, it may take a lifetime, or in some cases the vision is carried out by the visionary's successors after his or her death.

Vision is really about provision, not just for the visionary but others who will receive the blessings of its actualization. With so many unmet needs and misplaced priorities before us today, there is a demand on us to work a plan that will bring our God-given visions into reality. Without vision people's lives are wasted or destroyed. Thus, each vision in the scheme of God's plan is vitally important and must not be taken lightly.

With few "vision doctors" identified to help in the deliverance of needed visions, some of us must take on the role of the midwives of the past, who made house calls to insure safe and healthy deliveries of new babies. Most people and the whole earth travail, waiting on the manifestation of those chosen for this task. But will we escape from ourselves long enough to lend a helping hand to those crying loudly and silently around us? Perhaps their cries have been drowned out by our own personal cries for vision fulfillment.

Wherever you are in the process of living your vision and purpose, know that if you have conceived it, you must believe it and take the necessary steps to achieve it. The first step will be to pray and spend quiet time with God, so you can get in touch with your true personal identity–who you are, who you are in relation to the Lord, and why you are here. Then, you will want to write a personal vision plan for your life. Next, you will write a purpose statement that tells your reason for being, which includes how you will serve the Lord and help his people on this earth. Understand that God does not give a selfish vision. Finally, set goals and objectives, which are the mandatory practical steps that must be taken to fulfill your vision.

Remember, as you plan and work toward your vision, stand steadfastly on tried and true principles of integrity. These principles can be found in the Bible and other good books of instruction and in role models. Most of all, God–the giver of righteous vision–should be glorified. His integrity should be exemplified through the visionary and his or her staff members, affiliates and associates. Prayer, committed people, money, buildings, programs and other resources contribute greatly to the success of a vision but cannot replace virtues like honesty and just simply treating people with respect and kindness.

"Commit to the Lord whatever you do, and
your plans will succeed." - Proverbs 16:3 NKJV

Expanding Capacity with Vision

No God-given vision is too great to realize. Although many human aspirations seem lofty and too impractical to manifest, the truth is, we can attain what we envision, especially if it is divinely bestowed. Our spiritual capacity extends far beyond our natural grasp. A great part of our capacity to understand spiritual matters is still unused. The truth is: we are spirits who possess minds and live in bodies. So the supernatural is not only available to us but it is who we are–spirits.

What each of us can eventually find is that as we pursue vision, personal traits and values come to the forefront. An unfolding of character, potential and purpose emerge from within. Just as the brilliance of gold shines after much heat and pressure, so does the person who cooperatively goes through the process of character refinement.

The rigorous testing experienced while pursuing a vision reveals strengths and weaknesses of the visionary, and can uncover layers of misconceived perceptions of oneself and the world. We are designed to explore and consequently grow and mature. Also, others must take part in the vision, particularly in areas where we are lacking. So the vision is about God, you and others; but mainly about you as it relates to character-building and the ultimate aim of your perfection.

Vision is actually a glimpse of reality already in the mind of God to be navigated into the earthly realm by the person in whom He has entrusted it. Then recipients of this blessing–through vision actualization–will be impacted by it. God's ultimate intention for giving us vision is to bless as many people as possible. Vision is ammunition to shoot down the destructive forces that are loose in the world. This is why "without a vision, the people perish." They have no offence or defense. Dr. Martin Luther King, Jr. understood this principle and did what he could to ensure that his dream and vision was shared with others. And now America is still benefiting from his vision, which inspires hope in people throughout the world.

Dr. King was infused with a vision that moved him to fight for the civil rights of his people and the human rights of all people. The status quo American government and leaders of the day did not hand over civil rights to African Americans upon Dr. King's first, second, or third request. But only after Dr. King was threatened, sprayed by fire hoses, attacked by dogs, spat upon, mistreated and jailed, did legal victory come. The signing into law of the Civil Rights Act 1964 was the triumphant outcome. His passion for freedom and justice outweighed any fear of death he might have had, for he was willing to give his life for it.

> **What each of us can eventually find is that as we pursue vision, personal traits and values come to the forefront.**

What drives you? What is your passion? Is it divinely inspired? How do you see yourself? What legacy will you leave for future generations? These are just a few questions that should be answered in order to fulfill your vision and purpose.

"For I know the thoughts that I think toward you, says the Lord, thoughts of peace and not of evil, to give you a future and a hope."
- Jeremiah 29:11 NKJV

Taking the Limits Off

New annual opportunities are fresh for picking when recognized by the young at heart. Dare to peek around the corner of problems, circumstances and perplexities to see beyond personal perceptions and emotions into the realm of ideas, dreams, and visions. For most, doing this is too much to even think about, it doesn't make sense, and it's too dreamy for the real world. But consider that all that we purchase and consume started with an idea, a dream or a vision and was packaged for appeal to sell. Moreover, just think, some things conceived and brought to term are so valuable and priceless they cannot be bought or sold. Whether marketable or not, the point to grasp is: the end product was not aborted in the idea or embryonic stage.

Let's give life a greater expression by taking the limits off. First, take the limits off God because with Him all things are possible. Second, take the limits off our thinking. Conceive to achieve. As a visionary, when I was told by one of my elders, "Take the limits off," I had to examine my thinking. Although, I was moving in faith, I had limited my expectations to what seemed probable to me based on past experiences. I had to begin seeing problems as opportunities to expand and exhaust my problem-solving capacity, so that God could step in and make impossibilities possible. This freed me to move beyond my limitations.

Liberation from debilitating limits may take strategic, even child-like optimistic thinking.

Once there was a little 4-year-old girl who had super-careful, fearful parents who told her so many things she could not do, she never knew what she could do. For instance, they told their over-protected daughter to never touch the piano because she might hurt her fingers and to never sing because she might lose her voice. She wasn't ever allowed run because she might accidentally fall.

For two more long years, she lived only in her parents' limitations until one day she decided, "Since I've become an expert in limiting myself, now I can begin to limit limitations. My parents will be so proud of me." So, while at school and before her parents came home from work, she started the process of taking unnecessary limits off.

She liked how she felt so much when she decreased her limitations that she took on a limitless attitude. As a result, she achieved beyond her wildest dreams. She played the piano, became an accomplished vocalist and a track star. Her parents couldn't help but be proud of her. At a banquet given in her honor because she had been labeled a genius and an exceptional young achiever, a reporter asked, "How have you done so much at the age of seven?" She replied, "I decided to let nothing block my progress. I just took the limits off."

Liberation from debilitating limits may take strategic, even childlike optimistic thinking. It is okay to relax, get rid of old baggage and "go for it!" Regardless of what we have or have not attained, there is so much more inside that must be brought out and shared with those around us and with the world. Attitude is one of the greatest factors that determine altitude.

Research and list the steps that must be taken to realize your dream. Begin now. Observe and learn from the youthfulness of children. Perhaps this is why Ecclesiastes 4:13 states, "Better is a poor and wise youth than an old and foolish king who will be admonished no more." Everyone should assume a disposition for learning, no matter how young or old.

"Assuredly, I say to you, whoever does not receive the
kingdom of God as a little child will by no mean enter it."
- Mark 10:15 NKJV

Testing Grounds

Pursuing a vision, building a business, or nurturing a life are acts of faith designed to challenge, perfect and fulfill us. You see, doing always affects being; although, it is necessary to be before we do. "...Be steadfast, immovable, always abounding in the work of the Lord, knowing that your labor is not in vain in the Lord" (2 Corinthians 15:58). Each human being is important, whether he or she realizes it or not. Being is the major breakthrough into life. The water breaks before a human life is birthed. Being makes all other things possible. Dominion was divinely bestowed with being.

What can we learn from focusing on these basic principles of life? Law and order are already established. It is just a matter of flowing with or fighting against divine providence. When ambition rises in a person, success can only follow when established principles and order are applied.

Within each trying experience, a character-building lesson can be learned. Faith, patience, endurance, humility, obedience, and a host of other virtues or qualities, if given the chance, can emerge to temper and mature our characters. It is our choice how we handle problems, hassles, set-backs, perplexing situations, and insults–spiritually or carnally. To be spiritually minded means life and peace but carnality guarantees unnecessary suffering. But how does one become spiritually-minded to deal with challenges wisely? First, go back to the Source of all knowledge, wisdom and understanding, the Almighty God. Pray for help and guidance and remember to ask God for forgiveness as well as anyone we have wronged. This opens one to receive spiritual blessings and to grow. Then, the next step is right action, which puts faith in motion and brings it to life. For faith without works is dead.

Be aware that testing occurs continuously during life through thoughts, actions, interactions, relationships, and decisions. Just as students are tested at each grade level, we are tested at each plateau of progress to which we excel in life. What is most critical to understand is that lessons are repeated over and over again until they are learned. So as lessons are learned, we are released to move on to a higher plane of operation.

What is most critical to understand is that lessons are repeated over and over again until they are learned.

When we give place to rebellion, jealousy, greed, lying, cheating and other sins, then troubles, suffering, and chastisement occur again and again until we choose to do what is right. Otherwise, one can continue to go through a revolving door and never live his or her purpose or experience fulfillment.

Therefore, let's think about where we are in life and why. Understand there is a reason for our current experiences–pleasant or unpleasant. Decide today to make the most of them all, grasping each message and applying it with wisdom.

"The testing of your faith produces patience. But let patience have its perfect work, that you may be perfect and complete, lacking nothing. If any of you lacks wisdom, let him ask of God, who gives to all men liberally"... - James 1:3-5 NKJV

Identifying Advantages:
The Enlightenment of Recognition

> **Life is the greatest gift and unveils the most amazing discoveries.**

Arise! Opportunity awaits you! It's a new day! Visible and camouflaged opportunities and opposition surround us, waiting to be seized. It is the perfect season to move forward, walking in the newness of life, stirring our gifts of God within and using them like never before. Some gifts and talents that have been dormant for years can now be activated as God pours out His Spirit on all people. So watch, pray, work and love in order to receive and release the blessings of this magnificent hour. Get in the flow and the move of God now while the getting is good.

Positioning is key. Acquiring our domain for fulfillment requires each of us to find our rightful place and function effectively in it. Those who submit to God and receive divine directions will be able to fulfill their higher purpose before leaving this earth. Of course, all will not, as evidenced in the evils that are manifest in this world today. But know that the challenges from the wicked work for the good of the righteous because God is sovereign.

Renowned author, Dr. Mike Murdock, founder of Wisdom Training Center, affirmed the value of an enemy when he said, "You will only be remembered for the enemy you confront. You will only be rewarded for the enemy you conquer. Enemies reveal your limitations and that forces you to pursue the gifts hidden in those near you. What God didn't give you, He has stored in someone near you and love is the secret code to the treasure."

As proven for the wise, challenges and enemies bring promotions. Knowing this great reality, we can rejoice. With the attitude of joy comes strength and victory; obstacles are transformed into stepping-stones and opportunities.

Revelation adhered brings transformation. Hearing, seeing, and understanding truth transforms an individual by renewing the mind. The Lord Jesus said, "Seeing they may see and not perceive. And hearing they may hear and not understand." So knowing this, do not be frustrated by the spiritually deaf and blind. Just keep moving in the light and darkness will never comprehend it. Keep in mind and heart that there are still hidden treasures (revelatory wisdom with all-encompassing prosperity) in secret places yet to be discovered by those who hold the light of truth.

Life is the greatest gift and unveils the most amazing discoveries. The mysteries that surround life are profound. With life's multiplicity of lessons and messages, there is always something else to learn.

"Forgetting those things which are behind and
reaching forward to those things which are ahead, I press
toward the goal for the prize of the upward call."
- Philippians 3:13-14 NKJV

Nurturing Greatness

History is constructed through the fulfilling of purpose. A close study of the lives of pioneers, pathfinders, and history-makers will reveal challenges they had to overcome. Such an observation provides a greater understanding of what it actually took for heroes and "sheroes" to carry out specific tasks and missions. There is much labor and sacrifice that accompany greatness.

The ongoing challenge is to be effective in areas we operate and live. Empowerment is only realized when we learn how to create and utilize tools to build better lives for themselves and others.

Our sphere of influence expands as we recognize, nurture, and use not only our gifts but also the gifts in others.

Each individual is divinely designed to carry out a specific mission but must answer the call that tugs the heart. Deep down inside there is something that others need which each individual has, and the challenge is to stir it until it rises to the surface and overflows in expression. And make no mistake, it takes courage to rise up and answer one's call. Also, keep in mind that many people carry out their missions behind the scene. The key is seeking, discovering, being oneself and moving into the position for which he or she was created to serve in. Everyone, great or small, was created to serve in some capacity.

Our sphere of influence expands as we recognize, nurture, and use not only our gifts but also the gifts in others. The opportunity to nurture and develop is all around us. Each new birth is a major occurrence. Whether it is the birth of a baby, a vision, or a nation, the dynamics of nurturing and developing must be activated for healthy growth and maturity to take place. One broken bond or single evil seed can affect the fate of hundreds, thousands, and even millions of people. Thus, each child is precious.

So, it is the responsibility of parents, guardians, teachers, visionaries, and the heads of state to provide for and protect person(s) or thing(s), which have been entrusted to them. Good stewardship is critical to the realization and fulfillment of purpose. Human suffering is perpetual because of malfunctions and breakdowns in individuals, families, communities and governments. Most of the disheartening situations witnessed today are the results of someone's shirking, avoiding, or "dropping the ball" of responsibility.

Yet, no matter what is occurring around us, we have the power to focus intensely, engaging ourselves in meaningful activities, which produce fruitfulness. When God said, "Be fruitful and multiply," He meant it to be in more ways than one. Babies, visions, and nations come forth through us, and what we do with what we have been given determines our destinies.

"... Be fruitful and multiply; fill the earth and subdue it; have dominion ... - Genesis 1:28 NKJV

Achieving Against the Odds

The privilege of living in this exceptionally dynamic era is a blessing to maximize. Look in any direction, including inward, and take notice of awaiting potential and new developments on the horizon. Excitement is in the air, so ride its wave with gusto. Be willing to bury all that is dead and grasp life like never before because this is our season to make history, building a steady bridge in the present to cross over into the future.

The mood and atmosphere charge with creative power to induce the births of many visions and the fulfillment of those already born. Time's rhythm seems to have increased, causing a sense of urgency in people with a burning desire to realize their dreams and accomplish all God purposed for them during this lifetime and beyond.

So, let us move ahead innovatively. What advantages have not been taken? What possibilities have not been considered? Are there talents and gifts unidentified or unused? A full supply of all that we need has either been deposited in the earth or is stored by the windows of Heaven, ready to be poured upon us through the activation of faith.

Consider those before us, who took what seemed to be little and made much of it. Frederick Douglass, the great abolitionist, began as a little enslaved boy who could not read, and became a great abolitionist, orator, writer, diplomat, and United States Marshal. Ida B. Wells, born to enslaved parents, became an outstanding journalist and publisher for freedom and justice in the late 1800s. She published articles about the lynching of African Americans, and other hate crimes and injustices. Maggie Lena Walker, born into poverty, became the first American woman bank president.

> **Meeting challenges enthusiastically opens our creative channels for the flow of workable solutions.**

Legacies of this type continue to be created today. Dr. Benjamin Carson, started his education as a failing student but became an acclaimed neurosurgeon. Wilma Mankiller, a young Native American, who worked tirelessly for the rights of her people, became the first woman chief of the Cherokee nation in 1985. These and others, too numerous to name, pressed through with zeal to get things done and to fulfill purpose.

One of the traits these great men and women had in common was problem-solving. As problems grip the world, know that with God, we have the ability to solve them. Complex situations arise to challenge and refine us. Meeting challenges enthusiastically opens our creative channels for the flow of workable solutions. This pushes us into the overcomer's realm of operation, where quitting is not an option; the place where, according to the Bible, "The Red Sea" parts, the wilderness is exited, and "The Promised

Land" is possessed.

Whatever it is that we are striving to achieve, the questions are always: "Do we want it badly enough?" and "Are we willing to pay the price?" If both of these inquiries can be answered with a resounding, "yes!" then, one can proceed victoriously toward his or her vision, dreams, goals, and objectives.

"The desired accomplishment is sweet to the soul."
- Proverbs 13:19 KJV

Part 2

OTHERS

Healthy Relations

Chapter 4

CULTIVATING MEANINGFUL CONNECTIONS

Getting an understanding of why we are connected to certain people helps us to treat them appropriately. Cultivating a meaningful connection can produce a relationship that heightens the quality of life, while negligence or abuse yields the opposite. This chapter aims to stir a healthy appreciation of people with whom we live, work, share space, or frequently communicate.

Valuing Relationships

Life is based on relationships. Our main purpose for existing is to relate lovingly and uniquely to our Creator and to each other. And here is the greatest challenge and test: to love the Lord your God with all our heart, soul, mind and strength; and to love your neighbor as yourself. Anything of significant purpose that one does is linked to some kind of meaningful relationship. This is why our lives are so impacted by others, especially parents, family, teachers, friends and peers. The need to love and be loved is

> **Anything of significant purpose that one does is linked to some kind of meaningful relationship.**

43

an innate longing within that produces many actions and reactions, positive and negative, towards self and others.

Learning the art of good relations can be a lifetime quest. It requires a willingness to give and to forgive continually. This can cause many to lose heart and give up on people who do not have the wisdom or strength to reciprocate love. This type of discouragement and disappointment causes divorces, family breakups, and terminated friendships. Yet, when we watch the effective workings of good relationships, love, respect and trust for one-self and others from each person comprises the premise on which they are built. Therefore, each one is responsible for doing his or her part.

In this life, parents or guardians have to pay a great price for abandoning and abusing children with whom they have been entrusted. Fathers and mothers cannot abandon or abuse children and escape the penalty of their unwise choices. Nor can a husband or wife mistreat a spouse and leap into another marriage, peacefully blessed without settling all unfinished business of the prior union. If he or she does not deal honestly with personal faults and character flaws, that baggage is carried into the next relationship and can evolve into a depleting, vicious cycle.

Unhealthy cycles can be broken through honesty, prayer, and a commitment to change personally, for we cannot change others. Self-improvement means relationship enhancement. Since we have attracted people who have many of our own traits or the opposite but "packaged" differently, it is smart to look at them less critically and more inquisitively. One valid question to ask is, "Why did I attract this person into my life?" The answers discovered can be amazing. So, let's keep an open mind and a positive attitude for learning all we can.

"Two are better than one, because they have a good reward for their labor. For if they fall, one will lift up his companion." - Ecclesiastes 4:9-10 NKJV

The Gift of Life

Life. How precious it is ... an irreplaceable gift. With it we get breath, spirit, energy, intelligence, movement, order, growth and host of other benefits. Thus, our capacity to create and accomplish is as expansive as we can envision and reach. Every minute of life embodies possibilities beyond measure. A mere momentary decision can change the whole course of one's life and destiny. We, humans, sit on the brink of such tremendous breakthrough while toiling with our own perceived limitations. In fact, the toil within, the mental battle, is our greatest challenge.

> **A mere momentary decision can change the whole course of one's life and destiny.**

Even when the desires of one's heart are obtained, there is always something more to be desired. The human appetite for more can be a blessing or a curse but we need not let greed invade us or complacency bind us. God has provided enough resources in this world for us. Although it appears that the competition may take our portion of the pie, there are plenty of pies in disguise just waiting to be taken; whole pies, not portions. Abundance comes when one ingests the reality of provision for the whole. In other words, look at the whole organism of this creation. When life is given, every living creature is provided the basics for living mentioned earlier. What we do with these gifts is up to each of us individually, then collectively.

As awesome and beautiful as life is, the search continues for meaning and direction. By detecting the richness of each one's uniqueness and talent (especially in children), some of the suffering that comes with not knowing oneself and one's purpose could be avoided. Youth and adults would have little reason to rebel through devious behavior. Crime would decline to an all-time low. Productive creativity would escalate to an all-time high.

"Life is more than food, and the body is more than clothing. Consider the ravens, for they neither sow nor reap, which have neither storehouse nor barn; and God feeds them. Of how much more value are you than the birds?"
- Luke 12:23-24 NKJV

The Love 'Man-date': Small Gestures Count

Just a little love goes a long way. Today, most people hurt within, perhaps never to be helped or comforted, because many of us don't take the time to do the small things that mean so much – a phone call, a kind word, a card, a smile, or a hug. For most people, any of these will do. The world without these nurturing gestures would be too much to bear. But thank God, love is alive and well. This most powerful force, synonymous with God, is at our disposal at all times. It is up to us to put it into action. As the saying goes, "Love is not love until you give it away."

Love is not love until you give it away.

Be encouraged this season to give love away more than ever. Let's think of creative things we can do to express the love that lies dormant in our hearts. Someone's life can be touched and changed by it for the better.

Not to get too mushy, but I'm talking about expressing love like never before. Wives, children, mothers, sisters, brothers, aunts, nieces, nephews, cousins, and friends are void of something very special when the love of father, head of family, is missing. So many men are missing from their roles in the home and culture; we all pay the price for absentee dads. Thus, the love of grandfathers, uncles, brother, and other male mentors is critical to the well-being of families, neighborhoods, and society as a whole.

Of course, love and appreciation should be lavished on the fathers and other male mentors who are standing strong with their immediate and extended families. Yet, we should not forget the ones who, for whatever reason, are not present. Pray for them, forgive them, and let go of all negative thoughts and feelings about them. This opens the door for positive change to occur. And don't forget to be patient.

> **Our character is built and perfected as we challenge ourselves to transcend higher than our opinions, thoughts, and feelings.**

Let's remember how longsuffering God is with us, before we give up on those who have strayed from blessed relationships, evaded responsibilities, and made unhealthy choices in general. Although we should not condone such behavior, neither should we condemn, point the finger or maintain an unforgiving attitude.

The power to heal emotional and mental hurts becomes ours when we submit to God and forgive. Our character is built and perfected as we challenge ourselves to transcend higher than our opinions, thoughts, and feelings to do what is right according to God's laws and principles.

"Love suffers long and is kind; love does not envy; love does not parade itself, is not puffed up; does not behave rudely, does not seek its own, is not provoked, thinks no evil; does not rejoice in iniquity, but rejoices in the truth ... Love never fails." - I Corinthians 13: 4-6, 8 NKJV

Seeing Through Illusions to Love

"Romantic encounters of the blurred kind" would be a great title for a TV series, movie or a book, but unfortunately it is a topic as real as life itself. Dating and mating can be confusing and disenchanting, especially when couples are confused about how to carry themselves and proper etiquette. In most cases, the way two people launch is the way they land. The desire for true love has gotten many love enthusiasts into trouble they wish they had avoided altogether. From the surface, perhaps the admirer thought that person was his or her type. Everything seemed so right but turned out so wrong.

> **Love is so wonderful and magnificent that even when it is not present, there is a tendency for those longing to be loved to counterfeit it for all intents and purposes.**

Certainly, there is vulnerability when man and woman, male and female are attracted and begin a relationship. Usually, it requires growing and maturing to maintain a relationship. There is simply a lot to learn. The lyrics of a popular song from the 1960s by Jewel Akins advocates the need to learn about love: "Let me tell you about the birds and the bees, and the flowers and the trees, the moon up above, and a thing called love." Yes, romance, as beautiful as it is, cannot sustain a relationship.

Beware of the optical illusions of life that appear so real. When the viewing angle of an object is altered or the object is moved, a whole new picture is seen. So, look beyond sex appeal, status and superficial compatibility. Find out more about who you are, really, and who that person is to whom you are attracted. Pray. Ask questions, like: what are your goals and vision for your life? What is your belief system and faith? What are you looking for in this relationship? Do you want a committed relationship? What are your strong likes and dislikes? Then, listen, observe and respond calmly without being judgmental.

Trust and commitment are the basic components of all healthy relationships.

If there are fundamentals that do not line up with who you are, and your values, consider if it is worth it to continue to see that person. It's better to end the relationship early on a good note than to have to end it later on a note of discord.

Trust and commitment are the basic components of all healthy relationships. With the divorce rate at an all-time high, we need to examine why so many people are uncommitted and/or inaccurate in their choice of mate. Love is so wonderful and magnificent that even when it is not present, there is a tendency for those longing to be loved to counterfeit it for all intents and purposes.

When things don't work out in male-female relationships, disappointment and sometimes depression may result. When someone repeats this type of experience over and over again, it's time for self-examination. To be cleansed of deception on all levels, we must erase all of our perceptions and preconceived ideas, then, prayerfully begin our ingestion of information (scriptures first) with a clear and open mind, and a willing spirit. This enables us to separate the real and lasting from the unreal and temporal. Only truth will set you free.

Whatever happened in our lives thus far has occurred for a reason. The question is: did we learn our lessons well in order to grow and avoid repeating them? Self-evaluation and accurate assessments are necessary to chart our courses and enthusiastically head in the right direction.

> *"You will know them by their fruits. Do men gather*
> *grapes from thorn bushes or figs from thistle?"*
> - Matthew 7:16 NKJV

Detecting Potential to Develop People

Discovering and using potential, especially in matters concerning education and learning as it relates to individuals and families, is paramount for the ongoing well-being of a society. Since God made each of us with great potential, it is no wonder most children and many adults do not know what to do with themselves and have frequently been described as "bouncing off the walls." Perhaps this is why the Bible teaches us to "follow after love and desire spiritual gifts" (1 Corinthians 14:1).

For each child that falls through the cracks of abuse, crime, drug addiction, alcoholism, poverty, and just plain ignorance, a severe price is paid by all of us. The loss of life and potential creates aches and pains in the atmosphere of creation that manifest in the forms of pressure, stress, and duress – a drain on our energy and potential. What affects one affects us all in ways we know and know not.

How can we escape the responsibilities of learning and teaching? Whether formal educators or not, each one can teach one something of value. Maybe we have become too distant to reach ourselves, making it impossible to reach others. During a lecture in graduate school at the Ohio State University, I recall a renowned psychologist and professor, Dr. Linda James Myers, saying, "Self-knowledge is the basis of all knowledge." It is important to understand that when knowledge of the inner self is not learned, other forms of knowledge and social programs cannot reach the core of human issues.

Through the maze and rush, busy days turn into weeks, weeks into months, months into years, and years into decades. Before we know it, potential is unused, people are abused; all the while, we hold the potential to change things. However, unless we pause to evaluate, assess, and seek direction from our Maker, we can easily bypass ourselves. We need, desperately, to find out who we really are – who God made us to be– and be our true selves.

Untapped potential to touch, to love, to nourish and to conquer lies dormant on the shelves of our minds and hearts, waiting to be activated.

The world, with all its natural wonders and splendor, provides therapeutic environments. The beauty of the blue sky, the glowing moon, sparkling stars, the rising sun, blooming flowers, towering mountains, flowing streams and rich horizons, when aesthetically appreciated, can provide just the right atmosphere for getting in touch with ourselves and our Maker.

There are other environments created by man that are not so conducive to healthy human development. In the midst of pollution, tall skyscrapers, ghettoes, and traffic jams, a great amount of human potential can be choked and stifled. Even breathing can become a major risk. It is no surprise that people are getting physically sick and mentally, spiritually, and emotionally depleted. The external realm where most people are aimlessly searching is a cold and lonely place. Only in the inner environment of the mind and spirit can true peace and clear identity be found–the sanctuary where our Creator abides. Yet, this is not taught in most homes and public schools.

Most messages that are sent through television, video games, music videos, and so on, do not ignite a desire to learn (especially about self) in many of our children. More emphasis is placed on the external –what looks good to the eye, feels good to the body, and feeds the arrogant ego. Children simply respond by learning this lustful, rebellious, and even violent behavior. The misuse of electronic technology is costing us lives each day.

Regardless of how grim conditions appear, hope is still alive and well. Untapped potential to touch, to love, to nourish and to conquer lies dormant on the shelves of our minds and hearts, waiting to be activated. "For we are more than conquerors through Him that loved us" (Romans 8:37). We can do it. We should do it. We must do it–create a burning desire to stir up good potential within ourselves and others.

"Stir up the gift of God which is in you."
- 2 Timothy 1:6 NKJV

Chapter 5

DEVELOPING A HEART TO BLESS

We were created blessed and to be a blessing. God's original intent for making us was motivated by his great love for us. He blessed us with the gifts of life, love, intelligence, and creativity, so we could be like Him, have dominion and help fellow humans. Plus, the Sovereign King of all creation desires to enjoy an intimate relationship with each of us.

Divine Help for Getting It Right: The Way We Treat One Another

While spiritual and technological advances make this period a most progressive and exciting time to live, it is also a more pressured and tense era. Pertaining to these last days, the Almighty states in the scriptures, "I will pour out My Spirit on all flesh; your sons and daughters shall prophesy; your old men shall dream dreams, your young men shall see visions" (Joel 2:28 NKJV). This describes a new level of the Lord's grace being poured out on us–a spiritual or supernatural download from above.

On the other hand, disrespect, dishonesty, scandals, overpricing, fraud, abuse, violent assaults, murder, and other crimes are escalating and will be unbearable for many emotionally fragile individuals and families, especially those who do not believe in or know God. During extremely hard times, many will discover that mental, emotional, and spiritual stability can be secured only through a strong relationship with God.

> **During extremely hard times, many will discover that mental, emotional, and spiritual stability can be secured only through a strong relationship with God.**

Modern psychologists, psychiatrists and clergy have diagnosed and labeled our society as "sick." And when we observe the behavior of many parents, children, community, business, government and church leaders, can we refute their ill prognosis? It would be good if we could, but let's face it, something has definitely gone wrong at the very core of human development in family relations. Of course, a positive attitude will help: however, again, only steadfast and divine communion will provide the courage and strength to carry on in the midst of a chaotic world. Peace absolutely must be found within through a close relationship with God.

Check out the heart first. Is there any trace of unforgiveness, hatred, envy, jealousy, covetousness, lust or the likes residing inside? Are petty differences such as race, gender, class, position or religious denomination still hindering us from working together for the good of all? Does a superior or inferior self-attitude prevail within? If even a trace of any of the above traits is rooted within, please understand that one cannot be ready. We talk about cultural diversity, but how well do we really respect and understand other cultures? These are issues that will not disappear.

So let's consistently sit still in a quiet place, pray and allow God to touch our hearts, so we can heal and get divine directions for fulfilling our purpose now and hopefully during our lifetime. As we move in our purpose and help others to move in theirs, evil will ultimately be defeated and our change and victory will manifest to the glory of our Heavenly Father.

"Take heed, watch and pray; for you do not know when the time is. It is like a man going to a far country, who left his house and gave authority to his servants, and to each his work, and commanded the doorkeeper to watch. Watch therefore, for you do not know when the master of the house is coming ... lest, coming suddenly, he finds you sleeping. And what I say to you, I say to all: Watch!" - Mark 13:33-37 NKJV

Passionate Pursuit of a Worthy Cause

When a noble cause is converged with courageous action, divine purpose is fulfilled. There's nothing like a cause which time has come or a person whose hour of destiny has arrived. But this kind of dynamic interaction only takes place with a willing individual or group to ignite it. Such was the civil rights movement of 50s and 60s. It is an example of what can happen when God moves on the behalf of a people oppressed and they move with Him. But He looks for leaders of integrity whom He can use to move a people group or a nation forward. Such leadership was exemplified by Dr. Martin Luther King, Jr., civil rights activist and Nobel Peace Prize laureate, and Mrs. Rosa Parks, mother of the modern day civil rights movement.

The connection between Dr. King and Mrs. Parks was both life-changing and historical. Their synergy was that of a spiritual brother and sister with a linked mission. And it was a model to others in the movement, especially the students who became involved with sit-ins and protests for the civil rights we have today. Dr. King knew the precious value of Mrs. Parks and that without her, there might not have been a modern day civil rights movement. "To Rosa Parks, whose creative witness was the great force that led to the modern stride toward freedom," stated Dr. King, in the book, *Rosa Parks: My Story* by Rosa Parks with Jim Haskins.

> ## "The only tired I was, was tired of giving in..."
> ### - Mrs. Rosa Parks

For what cause do you stand? What are you passionate about? What problem bothers you profusely? Will you act or merely react along with the masses? Will you wait for someone else to do that for which you were born? To witness the scandals and lack of integrity surrounding many leaders today can be frustrating but means nothing unless those disheartened arise into their rightful place of leadership. If you see there is a void, something that needs to be done or created, why wait for someone else to do it?

Let it be known that Mrs. Parks was not physically tired the day she refused to give up her seat. "The only tired I was, was tired of giving in," said Mrs. Parks in her autobiography mentioned earlier. So, what happened on that bus in 1955? It was the result of many different experiences and observations of racism in her life and she was simply fed up. In 1995, during the Quiet Strength Tour, which commemorated the 40th anniversary of Mrs. Parks' refusal to give up her seat and the Montgomery Bus Boycott, she said something quite interesting. She told her international communications director, Beryl D. Anderson, when she was looking out of the window of that bus, she was thinking about her grandfather and Emmett Till, the youth who was brutally murdered by racists in Mississippi in August of 1955.

The courageous spirit shown by Dr. King and Mrs. Parks is alive and still moving today; ready to help us make a difference in someone's life. I can't help but think of late1800s and early 1900s' abolitionist and publisher, Ida B. Wells. Now, our time has come to meet the challenge and to pioneer new territory in every sphere of influence. It's comforting to know that God and heaven backs us, as well as all who are for justice, peace and righteousness.

As we march into the future with zeal and determination to live life in its fullest, let's continuously be inspired by the question: Is there not a cause? Certainly, there is for each of us. So, identify your cause and pursue it passionately.

"Do not strive with a man without cause, if he has done you no harm. Do not envy the oppressor and choose none of his ways."
- Proverbs 3: 30-31 NKJV

The Ties that Bind Us

Blessed be the ties that bind us. We are family – the human family. Family is a sacred institution through which all life begins and grows. Created in the image of our Creator, our potential far surpasses our current comprehension of our identity and purpose. Having been born into a nuclear family, given a name, nourished, sent to school, perhaps taken to church, we learned our ways and mannerisms–positive and negative. The powerful influence of family and environment is unavoidable and inescapable. Thus, the condition of a person's immediate family and surroundings directly affects his/her development. This is why the ties that bind us must be blessed in order not to be cursed.

As sung and spoken so truthfully in the lyrics by Peter Schickele –"No man is an island; no man stands alone." In spite of the fact that our society has become so individualistic, no one can function without the help or input of others. Self-made people don't exist. We desperately need each other. Like it or not, we are family. Yet, "we are all like sheep gone astray; we have turned everyone to his own way" (Isaiah 53:6). To leave our first loves – God and family – for unholy desires can only bring chaos that we see in our nation and the world today.

> **Self-made people don't exist. We desperately need each other.**

Thank God, we still have the opportunity to look in the mirror and make the change. Let's honestly challenge ourselves. Are we really helping others when we can? Are we making efforts to identify and correct our own faults before looking at the faults of others? Who are we really trying to please- ourselves, people, or God? Are there motives for the good deeds we do? If so, are they righteous or unrighteous? Each of us will have to search our own heart and repent, if needed, to come clean.

In whatever area of family advocacy we are lacking, efforts can be made to improve. We have been given the power to heal and to love, and the need is greater than ever. Children cry out for love and discipline first through misbehavior, then by total rebellion as they steal, kill, and destroy with no remorse.

Perhaps some have judged and mistreated certain people because of race or color, while others have lived in anger from feeling the pain of racism, oppression, poverty, and injustice. Some are imprisoned in self-hatred as others grip survival and live in despair. Consequently, there are so many unhappy people trying to fill the void of love in all the wrong places–bars, night clubs, street corners, video game rooms, casinos, gang life, shopping malls, and yes, on the corporate ladder of success. Yet, none of these can take the place of wholesome family love, which begins with love of self and God.

As much as our society stresses the importance of success, good looks, wealth and happiness, it doesn't nurture the prerequisites of "the good life." In fact, the "lasting good life" in which there is peace with self and God, came to me through accepting His grace through Jesus Christ. Now, I am secure that even after I die, I have eternal life. Are you secure concerning your future? Certainly, this world is too unstable and chaotic to offer true security or safety. Seek God.

"Love the Lord your God with all your heart, and with all your soul, and with all your mind. Love your neighbor as yourself."
- Matthew 22:37, 39

Using God-given Dominion Righteously

Within us is the innate ability to leap beyond mere survival to exceptional achievement. We are endowed with the faculties to think, reason, analyze, and spiritually discern what happens within, around and beyond us. Our spiritual and intellectual endowments, when developed, yield miraculous accomplishments.

The decision to use these divinely endowed gifts for good or evil has always been a personal choice. To be or not to be, to love or not to love, to have or not to have, are states of being that we have power to influence and change. Although the world conditions us to feel insecure and scared about our very existence, in reality God beckons us to stand secure and faithful, like He does, calling and working needed creations into existence. No one can be stopped or held back if they are awakened to this type of power and learn how to use it.

Connecting with our Maker is how our dominion is put into perspective. The highest purpose in one's life can only be fulfilled through deep soul-searching, discipline, and recognition of one's connection to God. How each of us relates to self, our Maker, and fellow humans constitutes our position in life. Since God is all-knowing, it follows that through communing with Him (within us) during introspective quiet time, we can be knowledgeable and wise. This being the case, no one should be ignorant. Yet, we know that ignorance and fear have set up camp on planet earth and are holding many people hostage with no ransom.

> **Our spiritual and intellectual endowments, when developed, yields miraculous accomplishments.**

Indoctrination, segregation, interrogation, and humiliation, are some of the world's weapons to intimidate and trick people into mediocre complacency. But before any of us think "Oh those poor people," realize that we all have encountered some nonsense along the way and perhaps have been sidetracked by it.

The key is to refuse to go along with any nonsense or foolishness. God's commandments and a relationship with Him is what counts. When we make our stand, trusting that God will stand within us, and we exercise the power of the written (scriptures) and spoken word, and then back it with positive action, something has to give. We can rejoice that when we do this, we become empowered.

"God has not given us a spirit of fear; but of power, and of love, and of a sound mind." - II Timothy 1:7 NKJV

The Blessing of Diversity

Who can figure out the mysteries that our Creator has not yet revealed, especially in regard to our distinctions and inter-relatedness? His infinite wisdom is all encompassing, beyond the grasping of mere human intellect. Why has God created so many people of all nations, creeds, colors, cultures, and customs and placed them all over this planet?

A message rings out from the masses of us as we live and have our beings in close proximity: we need each other and we're divinely designed to complement, challenge and help each other. Human intellect can reason differences subjectively, causing the attitudes of racism, bigotry, and discrimination to arise in the thought process. This narrow view limits the level of achievement of the human race, diverting our creative energy, which could be invested in developing our greatest resource – people.

> ... We are divinely designed to complement, challenge and help each other.

Racial differences can then be viewed as diversified and unique, created to be complementary just as a bouquet of flowers. The floral arrangement blends a variety of colors, designs, and aromas to make it extra beautiful and aesthetically enjoyable. Each race or ethnic group has unique gifts to contribute to the human family.

So we can see that nurturing relationships appropriately can make all the difference in the search for purpose and fulfillment. Consequently, this is an area where we encounter the most problems. Everything important in life requires the utmost attention and is critical to our well-being. This being the case, we all should make relationship healing and building our number one priority. Relationships with parents, siblings, relatives, mates, friends, colleagues, associates, and even enemies can be improved with prayer and communication strategies.

Since we cannot escape the inter-relatedness of our functioning as human beings, seeking to better understand the depth of this reality can help one discover incentives for loving fellow brothers and sisters. When any one of the gifts is withheld or suppressed, the family suffers some degree of dysfunction. The only way to avoid this is by helping each child to discover his or her purpose(s) and to grow up into it. Just think of how much crime and wasted potential could be eliminated.

The heartbeat of this world affects us all. What happens to the leadership of a nation, a city, a business, an organization, a church, or any entity affects the whole body of that entity. When the head is attacked, every member is affected in some way directly or indirectly. Selfish ambitions, greed, and hunger for power and control cause some people to develop disconnected consciousness, which produces destructive actions. In such cases, families and nations suffer needlessly. When one person is disrespected, God Almighty is disrespected. So, let's strive to set a better example for our children.

As we reach out to better relations with others, we inevitably improve ourselves.

... "If we love one another, God abides in us, and His love has been perfected in us." - 1 John 4:12 NKJV

Race Relations

What we perceive is not always accurate. Messages in the form of pictures, words, sounds, and vibrations are targeted at us each day via people, television, radio, social media, newspapers, and magazines. Some of the information is impressive enough to compel or provoke us to make assumptions, pass judgments, and draw conclusions. Other sensational messages even provoke weak and wicked souls to violence, racial division, and hatred.

The media coverage of news, world events, and issues does affect public and private opinions. As I reminisce about my study of "cameras in the courtrooms" as a journalism student years ago before TV cameras were allowed into hearings and trials, I can see now why I was suspect of it. Now there are channels dedicated to covering trials. TV coverage of the O.J. Simpson murder trial

> **Each race has special gifts to help all humanity.**

was extreme, to say the least. Hurting people in this real-life crisis were treated like actors in a continuous saga. Innocent or guilty, can defendants get a fair trial with so much media coverage?

Finally, the reading of the not guilty verdict caused all kinds of reactions. The media said a majority of Blacks were happy about the verdict, while a majority of Whites were unhappy. Well, what did they expect? America has a shameful history of legal slavery, Jim Crow laws, discrimination, and racism that has perpetuated ongoing divisions and distractions to deceive people from completing their higher missions.

The race of a person should not matter when it comes to justice or any other factor in life. In fact, race diversity is one of God's gifts to humanity, offering variety and beauty. Each race has special gifts to help all humanity. We all should feel good about who we are and the race we were born into. However, if we listen to popular rhetoric, inferiority and superiority complexes will invade us.

To cleanse ourselves from deception on all levels, we must erase all of our perceptions and preconceived ideas, then prayerfully begin our ingestion of information (scriptures first) with a clear and open mind and a willing spirit.

Optical illusions look so real. Yet, when the viewing angle on an object is altered or the object is moved, a whole new picture is seen. But why didn't we see it in the first place? Human beings will one day see the real picture of their lives, purposes, and destinies, asking this same baffling question – "Why didn't we see it in the first place?" However, we have the power to refuse a destiny of regret.

To live life effectively and purposefully, fulfilling our higher mission – to glorify our Maker and return to Him – we must have a clean heart created and a right spirit renewed within us. This can only be done through our Creator with our cooperation.

"Judge not that ye be not judged." - Matthew 7:1 KJV

People: The Greatest Resource

This fertile planet on which we abide has never ceased to produce and reproduce the raw resources that supply our needs and desires. The earth yields an abundance of natural resources: food, water, oil, gas, coal, wood, iron, copper, gold, uranium, and precious stones. When you consider by products, the list is virtually endless. These products are reaped from the earth, priced and sold in the world's market places.

Likewise, people have continued to reproduce their kind since God created them. Over seven billion people live in this world. Just think, if each person fulfilled his or her purpose, we could experience paradise as originally planned by our Creator. Unfortunately, the drive to obtain power, money, and "things" has gone to an extreme, causing material possessions to be valued higher than human beings in the minds and deeds of many.

Things are never more important than people.

It is time to re-price material stuff, for things are never more important than people. Racism, bigotry, greed, abuse, discrimination and hatred are the fruits of the deceived, those who have been blinded and are producing this destructive harvest. They have been "conned" by the devil to abuse one of the greatest gifts of all of God's creation – fellow human beings. In their minds and with their actions, they rationalize why they are "superior."

We all were "created equal with certain inalienable rights – life, liberty, and the pursuit of happiness." Thus, we should honor each other with love and respect. Constant violation of this love commandment creates a cold, hostile, and even violent environment. Let's examine ourselves personally to see if we are, in some way, feeding into or contributing to a poisonous environment.

Within each of us, where the Spirit of God dwells, is the place true freedom, peace, and justice can be realized and secured. Looking in all the wrong places outside of ourselves profits us nothing. Of course, balance is the key. It is imperative to continue to confront and conquer bondage, discord, and injustice outwardly as it manifests. But the inner battle must be won as well. Victory over one's self makes it possible to love people the way we need to be loved.

"Do unto others as you would have them do unto you." - Luke 6:31 KJV

Working Together for a Greater Harvest

The benefits of labor are multiplied when our efforts are combined. This truth is evident in our society today as we see major corporations merge, joining their efforts and resources to expand their growth and possibilities. Synchronized motion is a powerful force, whether between governments, corporations, organizations, churches or individuals. When entities and people move together, environments, of necessity, must change for better or for worse. The reality today is that people, places, things, and conditions are changing more rapidly than ever before.

Technology is merely an agent of change, while God is the Mastermind behind it all. What's new to people is outdated to God. Although computer hardware and software packages just keep on coming, it will never catch up with righteous spiritual intelligentsia (God's all-knowing mastermind) in the highest places. For, long ago, God said, "Let us make man in our own image, after our likeness, and let them have dominion" (Genesis 1:26). Our position of dominion is so empowering, that it is where the root of our problem with evil lies, and can only be handled constructively through obedience to God. Just as He told Adam and Eve, "But the tree of the knowledge of good and evil, you shall not eat of it; for in the day you eat thereof you shall surely die" (Genesis 2:17). So, unfortunately, man and woman chose to disobey, and we have had problems ever since. Yet, even in the midst of suffering and challenges, we have been blessed with the ability to create and to prosper spiritually, mentally, and materially.

However, it is only possible to realize and actualize our dominion potential by moving individually and corporately with the Spirit, regardless of how uncomfortable it may be to do so. Note, both individual and corporate movements pose some challenges. Individual movement in the Spirit presents one with a personal choice to move with the next changes God is ushering in or to cling to the old and familiar. Soul-searching self-examination must occur. It takes faith to step out on the waters of change in our lives, for there is an inherent fear of sinking. But that fear must be overcome by a daring step of faith.

Be encouraged by Isaiah 43:2, which reads, "When you go through deep waters and great trouble, I will be with you. When you go through rivers of difficulty, you will not drown! When you walk through the fire of oppression, you will not be burned up – the flames will not consume you. For I am the Lord your God, your Savior ..." Simply accept this divine reassurance and proceed. There is new ground to be plowed and harvested. Regardless of the emphasis on technology, people are still the greatest harvest. One must also be willing to respect authority on all levels, which is a requirement for effectiveness and success in achieving personal and corporate goals. Before advancement into leadership positions, we must be good followers.

Synchronized motion is a powerful force, whether between governments, corporations, organizations, churches, families, or individuals.

After individuals, at least those who will, make a committed choice to move with obedience in our calling, then it will be possible to unify for strategic corporate mobility for righteousness. At this level of motion, there is no room for insecurities, jealousy, envy, selfishness or the likes. Moving with corporate vision requires all to have the same common goal – pleasing and glorifying our Maker as we help our fellow brothers and sisters. In order to be a part of "the big move" one must submit completely to the will of

God, denying self. Self-denial is the greatest test of character and spiritual maturity.

This time in which we live requires maturity. Lack of wisdom and discretion can cost a person to lose family, marriage, children, and even his or her life. Let us focus in on what is really important and not be sidetracked by distractions that consume valuable time, causing unproductive and excessive indulgence.

Keep in mind that the investments of today determine the returns of tomorrow. The harvest is truly plentiful.

"For the man who uses well what he is given shall be given more, and he shall have abundance. But from the man who is unfaithful, even what little responsibility he has shall be taken from him."
- Matthew 25:29 TLB

Part 3

CHANGE

Flowing with Transition

Chapter 6

MAKING LIFE ADJUSTMENTS

Flexibility is a requirement for making smooth transitions in life. But to be pliable, a deliberate effort must be made. Attitude, sacrifice, patience, and wisdom are traits that accommodate effective transitions. In this chapter, we present strategies to assist us during trying times of change.

Changing Life Cycles Gracefully

Old endings and new beginnings can be challenging, trying and/or refreshing. As another page or chapter of our lives unfolds, it is necessary to make adjustments and learn in order to progress through loftier levels of experience and achievement. Out with the old and in with the new is the order of this modern day. There are so many shifts and changes in the way we do things. Technological, psychological, and spiritual advances that were destined long before our time are ushering in transitions that practically force us to grow and develop or be left behind. Cycles through which we evolve are purposed to mature us and prepare us for a higher, broader, and deeper experience.

It does not have to be the end of one calendar year and the beginning of another to experience new cycles. Graduations, marriages, the forming of new teams, partnerships and friendships, moving to another residence or city, a change of career, an expansion of business, the birth of a baby; and sadly, the death of a loved one, friend or colleague bring changes and challenges. These are all new beginnings that require faith, strength, and flexibility on our part.

The decisions we make and what we do from one phase of life to another, determine our progress and growth. With the exception of God Almighty, nothing and no one stays the same. We either change for the better or worse. Our choices are critical because the decisions we make today bring the results we get tomorrow. And actually, what we are experiencing right now is the manifestation of seeds we sowed days, weeks and years ago. Knowing this spiritual truth, it seems wise to assess our current situations with the commitment to start afresh, initiating or planting for the future harvest we desire in our lives.

Maintaining balance during transitions requires discipline and focus.

The way we handle change determines how we progress. As the old fades away, the new is on the horizon. Outdated methods must give way to smarter, quicker and more modern means. Such is the rhythmic pace of daily living. Yes, change, whether sudden or gradual, can make our lives uncomfortable, unstable and unpredictable. Therefore, creative innovation tempered with graceful adaptability, are precious traits to nurture. But know that these admirable characteristics are rooted in faith, which enables one to see beyond circumstances. The appearance of deficiency, however it manifests, may only be dormant faith held hostage by fear.

Bound faith can be released with the keys of courage through the power of prayer, the spoken word of God, and a refusal to give up. Such tenacity will alter the chemistry of any environment, spurring into motion the elements of positive change – hope, inspiration and motivation to move on.

Maintaining balance during transitions requires discipline and focus. Sometimes deceptive surface appearances can distract and sidetrack us. This is why it is imperative to develop discretion, apply wisdom, and be not dismayed by threatening situations. Keep in mind that quick occurrences can easily create optical illusions, just as animation seems to bring still cartoons to life. It has been proven repeatedly that the hands are quicker than the eyes. Thus, in most cases the old adage is true – all that glitters is not gold. Also, consider that all gold does not glitter but must be heated, refined, molded, and polished.

> **The decisions we make and what we do from one phase of life to another determine our progress and growth.**

In reality, we are all like gold in the process of refinement. We are tempered and molded by the fires of change fueled by challenges, tests, trials and tribulations. And like medicine, that which we dislike most, is best for us. Just think, without change and challenges, potential would never be realized nor purpose fulfilled. So, we have all we need with which to work–the tools of faith, vision, creativity and persistence, which are sharpened through communion with God and study of the scriptures.

So, embrace the seasons of change with joy and renewed strength, knowing the gift of life opens a whole world of possibilities. Who can say with certainty what will happen tomorrow? Therefore, the wisest choice is to not worry about it but get prepared by living today to the fullest. Be inspired to not only flow with change but when needed, to initiate it.

"To everything there is a season, and a time to every purpose under the heaven." - Ecclesiastes 3:1 KJV

Preparation for Progress

In this age of spiritual resuscitation, information and technology, visions are springing forth through willing people who dare to realize their higher purpose. An abundance of resources await our grasp while time moves swiftly to usher us into the future and eternity. A God-induced momentum is building in the atmosphere and environment, which is evidence that we are on the verge of a great transformation and must get prepared for challenge and change. "The single greatest power we have in the world today is change. The most reckless, irresponsible thing we can do is go on living our lives like we have for the last 10, 20 or 30 years. I cannot think of a more dangerous policy than the conservatism that exists in our country today," says Karl Deutsch, noted Harvard professor.

Yes, it is a new day in every way. The scriptures declare in 2 Peter 3:8, "... Beloved, do not forget that with the Lord one day is as a thousand years and a thousand years as one day." Hence, the new millennium is a new day; and if we start counting at the turn of time (B.C. to A.D.) that commenced at the birth of Christ, two thousand years (two days, spiritually speaking) have passed. This means we are now living in the third day or millennium.

How exciting and challenging! Just think, so much is available and coming to us. The opportunities and possibilities can be spirit-moving and mind-boggling to say the least. It is essential to narrow the paths we choose to tread and to stay on the main narrow path the Lord has chosen for us. "Because narrow is the way which leads to life and there are few who find it" (Matthew 7:13 NKJV). Help to stay on the narrow way comes as we pray, study God's word, listen, learn, discern, focus and act in love.

Preparation is essential for effectiveness in anything we do. Consid-

> ## The smallest action is better than the greatest intention.

er that the world's way of getting things done has evolved from simple procedures to complex technologies, stimulating and increase of people's stress levels. But God's way of executing tasks is much simpler. It is so simple, in fact, that in the midst of problems and complexities, one can easily overlook His powerful words of knowledge and wisdom etched in scripture for our use.

When we speak and affirm God's word in total faith with no doubt, we can cause the world's most intimidating forces to halt and submit to divine order and authority. So let's look ahead courageously and optimistically, knowing that our Maker has deposited within us all it takes to make our dreams and visions become reality but more importantly, His plans for us.

Therefore, move forward without hesitation with new ideas in the Spirit. Keep in mind the words of an unknown but wise author who wrote, "The smallest action is better than the greatest intention." Whatever we do, regardless of how small, know that lives can be impacted by it. So, let's be and do the very best we can.

"Prepare your outside work. Make it fit for yourself in the field; and afterward build your house." - Proverbs 24:27 NKJV

Chapter 7

PROACTIVE RESOLVE TO MOVE FORWARD

Get up and get going. Forward motion opens up opportunities and possibilities. In this chapter, you will be further prompted to put faith into action. So go on and make that extra push to press toward your destiny.

Exiting Your Comfort Zone

This new day is divinely availed for our creative input and use. Something so uniquely different distinguishes each 24-hour span that keeps life in the present filled with hope, possibilities, and golden opportunities to be discovered. This is what makes living now so exciting and challenging. It is our time to righteously influence and impact individuals, families, neighborhoods, cities, states, nations, and the world. Although this may seem difficult, with God's help, we can do it. And our involvement is critical.

Although there appear to be few solutions for broken families, failing school systems, crime-ridden cities, and terrorized nations, we were created to contribute to the solving of these problems. In fact, the manifestation of these troubles before us is to stir purpose within and drive us to take action.

I shall never forget an event I attended in Toledo, Ohio, where a large number of people assembled to hear a well-known and highly respected speaker. As the speaker got up to deliver the message of the hour, a woman entered the auditorium and was seated directly behind me. Well, as the speaker continued, the lady began to respond loudly with words like "amen" and "that's right," etc. She was so disturbing, until the people in that part of the audience became very irritated. It became obvious that the lady was mentally disturbed and something had to be done. But what was even more disturbing was that the whole section of people was looking to me to fix this situation. I was amazed because I was a visitor and most of them were a part of the hosting organization of the event.

> **Many times, situations occur that alter our plans and extract us out of our comfort zones. Realize they happen for a purpose. The test is in how they are handled.**

My assistant, who had traveled there with me, looked at me with weariness in her eyes, wondering if I would do something about the problem that this group was depending on me to solve. The look in my eyes confirmed that I was going to do something but she would have to assist me. Then, I turned, looked the mentally disturbed woman directly in the eyes and asked her, "What is your name?" She gave me her name and I asked, "Do you want to be helped?" She replied, "Yes." I spoke softly, praying for her, commanding the demons to shut up, go back into dry places and not to return.

Immediately she sweated profusely as demons left her. She calmed down and was silent the remainder of the evening. Those seated nearby looked at me with relief, nonverbally conveying their thanks. The key point is: someone had to do something–me. Of course, I did not feel like dealing with the problem and initially wondered why someone else would not resolve it.

I later realized that helping that disturbed lady was my purpose for attending that function. After the event, that lady thanked me and told me God had told her to attend the event because it would be her night of break-through and deliverance. She revealed that her family had been plagued with mental disorders for generations. I was able to further minister to her and give her instructions and scriptures for deliverance.

Many times, situations occur that alter our plans and extract us out of our comfort zones. Realize they happen for a purpose. The test is in how they are handled. There are various choices that can be made with every challenge. One can respond to any given set of circumstances with wisdom or foolishness, courage or fear, compassion or selfishness. Once made, these critical choices can navigate an individual to a greater or lesser destiny.

*"Therefore let us pursue the things which make for peace
and the things by which one may edify another."*
- Romans 14: 19 NKJV

Walking By Faith

Once we tap into the Source, resources are abundant. We are rich because our Maker has created and made all things well with built-in provisions. The mother has the milk for the baby just as the teacher has the lesson for the student. God has put so many resources at our disposal. First, we have life which opens up everything else. The fresh, cool and warm breezes; the bright shining sun and the air-cleaning, soul-nurturing rain are all rich resources available to us.

It is our choice to enjoy the smell and beauty of flowers, plants, and trees, or cuddle a precious child. Be thankful for health, strength, a mind to think and reason, and emotions to sense and express affection. Each of us has a spirit so resilient that even when hurt and broken, it can be renewed and born again to access a vast reservoir of divine blessings, revelations, and eternal peace. What more can we ask?

Well, most of us still have our lists of needs and wants, both material and spiritual, so much so that businesses today thrive on our excessive consumerism. Ministers stretch to meet the needs of hurting people by praying, counseling, and guiding them to the point that many people have become dependent upon the ministry more than upon God. The word of the day is "more" ... more money, more power, more technology, more love, more spirit, more miracles, more signs, more wonders. The demand is so great, it seems the supply is not enough. In reality, the supply is so great that we are blinded by its vastness. We sometimes can't see the forest for the trees; so are the perceptions of human beings.

> **In reality, the supply is so great that we are blinded by its vastness. We sometimes can't see the forest for the trees...**

The challenge is to move ahead by faith and not by sight. There is plenty all around us and within us. Yet, false perceptions of lack causes a grim deception. Then, that deception manifests through negative thoughts and words, unbelief, false illusions and appearances facilitated by fear and low self-esteem. In essence, in spirit, we have all we need. However, all we have will not work for us until we work with it. When the major life principal – use what you have first – is activated, slothfulness, laziness, mediocrity and poverty are crushed and dissipated.

Upon a solid foundation of faith we can create, build, and live abundantly. Although we do not know exactly what will happen in this life, our willingness to believe and strive keeps life mysteriously and interestingly progressive. The urge of wanting to see is meaningless and empty without believing. Surely, "faith is the substance of things hoped for, the evidence of things not seen" (Hebrews 11:1 NKJV). The application of faith is the heart of abundant living. Dare to sow the seeds and expect to reap the harvest, but only after tilling and watering the soil. The work we do to attain our goals and to live our purpose puts faith into action. For faith without works is dead.

"The earth is the Lord's and the fullness thereof;
the world, and they that dwell therein." - Psalm 24:1 KJV

In Step with Time

Living today is distinctly different than life was for our ancestors. While they operated with fewer civil rights and less conveniences, life was much simpler and less crowded with distractions. During those times, people tolerated more in marriages, families, and other relationships, as well as in society as a whole. Now, people's patience and tempers are shorter, divorces are quicker, and traffic is more stressful. Yet, our fast-paced, information-oriented environment provides us an opportunity to develop, grow, and mature through various life experiences in the context of modern challenges.

Swift advances in business and computer technology, digital electronics, and cellular and satellite communications advanced with us into this millennium, demanding that we learn quickly to troubleshoot and problem-solve or be left behind. The functions of political assemblies, church ministries, civic organizations, families, and individuals are greatly affected by the pervasiveness of technology. The best way to deal with all the necessary changes and hype is to, in the Spirit, plan and work wisely now. God is a planner, so in order to be effective, we must faithfully chart our courses.

As we look and plan ahead, it is wise to first reflect on our history. To know where we are going, we must know from where we came. Gaining a more enlightened perspective can be quite inspiring. Just thinking of the outstanding overcomers in history, in our families, and communities is enough to fuel the fire of ambition and purpose. Christ Jesus said, "Greater works than these shall he do" (John 14:12). Thus, each generation can potentially accomplish more, in spite of the particular situations and circumstances of their times.

Even babies of today seem to be more alert than babies of the past; and necessarily so, when you look at what they must deal with in this century. God equips us for the times in which we are born. For example, few young African Americans would tolerate slavery today. They would most likely rebel completely no matter the cost. Few Asian Indians and Africans would tolerate the colonialism of earlier centuries.

So we never have to worry about lapsing into the past. It is impossible. Although one could argue that history repeats itself, it cannot in the same context. Progression is the order. Regression is chaotic. Those who reach inward and put on their spiritual gear can deal with whatever happens in the future. We can do all things with God's help.

"For there is a time for every purpose and
for every work." - Ecclesiastes 3:17 NKJV

Turning Points

Turning points are necessary shifts of direction leading to our destinations. It is our responsibility to make the turns when it is time, so that we don't miss them and go miles off course to get back on track. Because life, as we know it, is changing so rapidly that one needs a solid foundation and good directions to avoid being lost.

Just as having a dependable vehicle, adequate fuel, good directions and paying attention to signs are mandatory for a safe journey to a desired destination, so it is with life. Those who have no vehicle are left with no means to get where they need to go in life. Life is so dynamic that it requires us to keep moving toward a destination. No movement or growth, no fulfillment. Either we move toward our destination or become distracted and delayed.

Either we move toward our destination or become distracted and delayed.

Viable vehicles are created by recognizing and developing gifts, talents and skills or by forming business, corporate, religious or other organizational entities. These vehicles are fueled with faith, prayer, determination, creativity, planning, teamwork, action and perseverance. With a dependable vehicle, fuel and directions, we are on our way.

Fortunately, we do have choices concerning life's journeys. Decisions must be made on which route to travel. What short cuts, if any, are there, and should they be taken? Once I traveled about 170 miles by car to Charleston, West Virginia, where I spoke at a conference. Since I had never driven to Charleston, I called a travel service agency for the best route to and from my destination, and pulled out my own map to chart my course.

I had to choose between two routes – the interstate or the highway. Although the interstate offered freeways which by-passed small towns and traffic lights, it was actually 50 miles and about 40 minutes longer than the highway route. I chose the latter to save time, mileage, and gasoline. Another consideration in my trip was that I traveled during daylight to Charleston and returned the next evening after dark. Interestingly, the choices I made to get to and from my destination safely are similar to the decisions I have to make daily in getting to and from where I need to go in life.

Our great advantage is that we are given opportunities to prepare for each new day and journey. There are lessons all around us waiting to be learned and applied to God's bigger vision or destination for our lives. As much as most of us desire to live successful lives, God has more in mind for us than we have for ourselves. However, we must seek His guidance and follow His directions if we desire ultimate success – eternal peace, happiness and prosperity beginning now.

Something as simple as a walk, an observation of nature, a trip on a plane or in a car can spring up wells of wisdom if we listen to God's wee small voice within. Prayer and reading the Bible can bring calm and stability that cannot be found at the shopping mall, a sports event, party, or any other external affair.

The two-fold question for each of us is "Where am I now in life and where do I need to go?" Whatever decisions made, we will live with them. So make wise choices to keep moving purposefully in the right direction.

"Trust in the Lord with all your heart, and lean not to your own understanding; In all your ways acknowledge Him and He shall direct your paths."
- Proverbs 3:5-6 NKJV

Equipped to Win the Battle

The greater the battle, the sweeter the victory! When a lot of problems are thrown your way at once, something great in your life and destiny is trying to emerge. Taking on the attitude of a good soldier will help tremendously. The faithful attitude of winning is an offensive stance that wards off the fiery darts aimed to defeat us.

I recall a major point of a very intriguing message I heard recently. "Get on the offense. Stop responding to the assaults of the devil and start strategically planning and making assaults on him to prevent the success of evil schemes," declared Dale Sides, an apostle, a teacher, author and spiritual warrior who has helped to deliver many out of bondage and oppression in India for the kingdom of God. What better time than this to take and offensive stance in life?

In these times of swift change and demanding transition, faith and courage are required virtues. The 21st century brought many national and international challenges linked to war, terrorists, natural disasters, political shifts, and more. The impact of pornography and its perverted crimes require offensive measures to confront and dismantle. Because if we do nothing about this despicable filth, I believe it will cause the demise of many nations of the world. The raping of children should not be tolerated. I'm writing against it because it is a destroyer of lives. But we must not be intimidated by this and other threats to our well-being.

Faith is the only real option that can conquer fear and free us from the vicious threats of danger and disaster. Yet, realize that all things happen for a specific purpose. Hurricane Katrina exposed the nakedness and shame of breached national priorities confused by the blurred vision of poor planning, classism and racism. Then "Rita" and many hurricanes, storms, and disasters that have occurred, although harsh, represented mercy because lives were still spared.

One lesson these "storming daughters" of Mother Nature taught us is to treasure our most valuable resource–people. But did we really learn as a nation, as a people, as a world? Certainly, if we did, we would know that the grace of God was with us as revealed in the low fatality rate in areas where property was demolished. So, let's continue to help the survivors of these natural disasters.

> **God has granted us resiliency to bounce back from almost anything, if we don't give up.**

Although, being human causes us to gravitate toward tangible things, when they are stripped away, it's best to have some faith and courage to make it through. For out of faith and the courage to move on, restoration will come. God has granted us resiliency to bounce back from almost anything, if we don't give up.

"Yet in all these things we are more than conquerors through Him who loved us." Romans 8:37 NKJV

Repositioning for the New Day

It's a new day! Blessed are we to see and experience the advent of a fresh season and millennium. Anticipation and expectation of this dawning era have dissolved into realization. Visible and camouflaged opportunities surround us, waiting to be seized. It is the perfect season to move forward, walking in the newness of life, stirring our gifts of God within and using them like never before. Some gifts and talents that have been dormant for years can now be activated as God pours out His Spirit on all people.

So watch, pray, work, and love in order to receive and release the blessings of this magnificent hour. Get in the flow and the move of God now, while the getting is good.

Positioning is key. Acquiring our domain for fulfillment requires each of us to find our rightful place and function effectively in it. Those who submit to God and receive divine directions will be able to fulfill their higher purpose before leaving this earth. Of course, all will not, as evidenced in the evils that are manifest in this world today. But, know that the challenges from the wicked work for the good of the righteous because God is sovereign.

A few years ago, at the International Third World Leadership Summit at Bahamas Faith Ministries in Nassau, Bahamas, the following wisdom was shared by Dr. Mike Murdock: "Without Goliath, David would have only been a shepherd boy." So as proved, for the wise, challenges and enemies can bring promotions. Knowing this, we can rejoice. With the attitude of joy comes strength and victory; obstacles are transformed into opportunities.

Revelation brings transformation. Hearing, seeing, and understanding truth transforms an individual by renewing of the mind. The Lord Jesus

> **Just keep moving in the light and darkness will never comprehend it.**

said, "Seeing they may see and not perceive. And hearing they may hear and not understand." So, do not be frustrated by the spiritually deaf and blind. Just keep moving in the light and darkness will never comprehend it. There are still hidden treasures (revelatory wisdom with all-encompassing prosperity) in secret places yet to be discovered by those who hold the light of truth. As in a few words of an empowering song written by Beverly Dwyer:

"It's time to lead the way. God's Spirit is upon us. We are growing stronger day by day. Dominion over all the earth is still the holy order..." The Church is comprised of those from every nation, who discover "the way, the truth and the life." The mysteries that surround life are profound. With its multiplicity of lessons and messages, there is always something else to learn.

"... Forgetting those things which are behind and reaching forward to those things which are ahead, I press toward the goal for the prize of the upward call of God in Christ Jesus. - Philippians 3:13-14 NKJV

Part 4

STABILITY

Establishing Discipline and Balance

Chapter 8

THE GROUNDWORK
OF SPIRITUAL DISCIPLINE

In this life, what appears is not always what it seems to be. Determining truth from propaganda can easily escape the masses. This chapter presents points to consider when viewing, listening to, and reading media news reports, programs, and messages. Also, it deals with intentionally exercising the power to choose what is allowed to invade our time and space.

Watch, Listen and Pray

Observation through the Spirit of the Lord is imperative for clear understanding. There is more to what we see and hear each day than appears to the naked eye and ear. We are swiftly approaching a time when discernment and discretion concerning all issues – personal, spiritual, business, social and political – will be required for peace of mind and mental stability. Case and point: as we watch the evening news and other television programs, listen to radio news and commentaries, and read the daily newspapers and weekly/monthly magazines; blogs, Twitter and Facebook messages, what is the wisest response?

Before answering, let's consider the seriousness of some of the issues confronting us today. The destructive dilemma of war, the disrespectful scandals and character assassinations, extreme hunger and suffering, shrewd tactics of the tobacco and other industries to promote the sale of unhealthy products, decline of public schools, juvenile crime, millions of abortions, accidents, natural disasters, tragedies–to name a few–are issues that concern us and our children. Oh, and occasionally, there is some good news added jokingly during the last few seconds of sign-off, but there are so few, I can't recall them. This is one reason we should handle and interpret media with wisdom and discernment.

The wisest response to what we see and hear through media is to watch, listen and pray. Of course, after elevating spiritually, we can simply use our intelligence and at the appropriate time, make an assessment in a way that does not damage our character. For instance, when I heard all the scandals about, then U.S. President, Bill Clinton, I had to be careful not to judge and condemn, look at who was making the accusations, pray and then discern.

Whether the allegations were true or false, negative talking and pointing the finger were low-life ways of responding to it. I was reminded of the adulterous woman whose accusers wanted to stone (John 8:3-11). Jesus handled what could have been a deadly situation with wisdom and compassion. He told the accusers, "He who is without sin among you, let him throw the first stone." Consequently, all of them were convicted in their conscience and left one by one, leaving Jesus and the woman alone. Then Jesus asked, "Woman, where are your accusers? Has no one condemned you?" She said, "No one, Lord." Then, he said, "Neither do I condemn you; go and sin no more."

When you point one finger, three point back at you. Also, the scriptures further puts self-righteous accusers in check. "The Lord knows how to deliver the godly out of temptations and to reserve the unjust under punishment for the Day of Judgment, especially those who walk according to the flesh in the lust of uncleanness and despise authority. They are pre-

> **...We should handle and interpret media with wisdom and discernment.**

sumptuous, self-willed. They are not afraid to speak evil of dignitaries, whereas angels who are greater in power and might do not bring a reviling accusation against them before the Lord. But these, like natural brute beasts made to be caught and destroyed, speak evil of the things they do not understand, and will utterly perish in their own corruption" (2 Peter 2:9-12 NKJV). The key is to never absorb the negativity or judge what you see and hear in news reports as absolute truth. Instead, pray to discern truth from deception.

Many people are completely confused with distorted perspectives. Some are depressed by what they perceive. God knows all the answers, so rely on Him for a clearer understanding, especially before you judge and draw conclusions. In fact, by going to God, we can understand a specific news story, why it happened in the first place, and what if anything can be done to help resolve the issue. If we can't help, we need to be quiet and leave it alone.

> *"A wise man's heart discerns both time and judgment,*
> *because for every matter there is a time and judgment."*
> - Ecclesiastes 8:5-6 NKJV

Embracing Discipline, Rejecting Distractions

The world with all its appeal and technology is changing in such a way that it has become more and more challenging to live a balanced and wholesome family life. Distractions come from seemingly every direction to deflect our attention from meaningful priorities to meager annoyances. The tools for communication – television, telephone, cell phone, e-mail, social media – are all good tools for communication but should be turned off or ignored at times to maintain focus.

Communion with God is the only way to stay on track with our purpose and mission. Distractions can diffuse or scatter our energy, causing mental and physical drains. However, interactions and encounters that feed the spirit – the inner person – help the energy to become centered, so that one can be appropriately directed in order to plan, create, and bring visions into reality through faith and work.

Simplifying life is a worthy endeavor for living prosperously today. While the 21st century age of information and technology avails some of the greatest opportunities in human history, it also invades us with the worst distractions and insults. One needs only to check his or her e-mails, texts, Facebook posts and Twitter tweets to discover this. I admit, lengthy conversations can be avoided through e-mails and texts but occasionally, there's something special about hearing a human voice.

Sure, we should be thankful for the conveniences of internet communications and information access, cell phones, voicemail, digital and cell phone cameras, etc. Yet, we should avoid being consumed by our consumption. Certainly, there is more meaning to life than this.

Self-indulgence and over-consumption are great deterrents of destiny. When thieves and robbers of precious time and energy come into our environments, we must tactfully dismiss or ignore them. Remember that they may come disguised and can manifest in the forms of electronic devises and food.

Watching TV, engaging in unproductive conversations, surfing the web aimlessly, over-eating, and a host of other habits are making many overweight and sluggish. So, let's trim the excess and sharpen up.

Whenever we become drained from negativity and too much dis-

> **When thieves and robbers of precious time and energy come into our environments, we must tactfully dismiss or ignore them.**

traction, it is then time to stop for a few minutes to regroup, collect our thoughts and refocus. There are different ways to do this. Sitting still in a quiet or secluded place, praying, deep breathing, reading the Bible or another good book can work wonders.

Sometimes a moment beholding the power and presence of God in nature is all we need to spark inspiration and renew strength. In the midst of busy days, time outs to focus and simmer our energies and thoughts can be therapeutic. On one of those busy days at the office, I recall having so much to do–complete *Purpose Magazine* for printing, close business transactions, and deal with taxes and accounting issues, to name a few items. The thought of all these and other responsibilities and duties were stressful to say the least, until I decided to take a different approach.

The weather was absolutely beautiful, so I decided to go out to behold the sunset. As I drove west that winter afternoon, the horizon exalted the gold and orange hues of the shimmering sun that glistened through the branches of leafless trees... I said, "God, You're awesome!" As that thought dominated my being, all the stress and anxiety left as a feeling of joy and rejuvenation arose from within.

"Let us lay aside every weight, and the sin which so easily ensnares us, and let us run with endurance the race that is set before us ..."
- Hebrews 12:1 NKJV

Seeking the Best

Beyond the sight of natural and tangible realities is the spiritual origin from which they emerged. All that we hear, see, taste, smell and feel magnifies our physical urges and needs while minimizing the presence of our spiritual nature. Herein is the dilemma and challenge faced by each of us–striking a balance between the physical or natural and the spiritual. Knowingly and unknowingly, the search for meaning in life is the paramount quest that can link us to purpose and destiny. How this major quest is pursued can be the difference between living one's purpose and just longing for it.

> **Knowingly and unknowingly, the search for meaning in life is the paramount quest that can link us to purpose and destiny.**

Ask, and it will be given to you; seek, and you shall find; knock, and it will be opened to you. This biblical principle, found in Matthew 7:7, works when faithfully and persistently applied in the spiritual and the natural realms. Still, the road leading to truth and fulfillment requires discipline and endurance. Vision, focus, and application of knowledge through wisdom with righteous motives are all part of the dynamics of carrying out our divine assignments on earth. But who will make the sacrifice to gain true purpose? This requires serving others in the unique capacity for which God created each of us.

To have and maintain peace in today's world, it is necessary to access a realm beyond what we experience through the five senses. This is a critical reality most challenging to those who look for meaning in life from pleasures and instant gratification that are quick and fleeting. Although it is important to have good, clean fun, lustful and unclean indulgences create problems far greater than resolvable by the natural means through which they come. Indeed, exposure of children to promiscuous and violent behavior via media, at home and in school, proliferate crime more and more within each succeeding generation.

There's really no need to expound upon each problem or issue prevalent in society since watching TV news reveals nearly all of them–wars, murders, scandals, substance abuse, diseases, etc. But what's so disheartening is the fact that genuine solutions seem unattainable, no matter how hard politicians, clergy, educators, parents, civic leaders, businesspersons, and others try.

The perplexities of the day and era test and try the strongest and wisest among us. But thank God, there's hope, answers, and attainable resolves. It doesn't take a rocket scientist to figure things out. Simply have faith in God, His word, and oneself with an openness to learn. Then, it is just a matter of applying the truth already available in the Bible.

"Walk in the Spirit and you shall not fulfill the lust of the flesh."
- Galatians 5:16 NKJV

Chapter 9

THE WORK-PLAY EQUILIBRIUM

The balance of work and play paves the road to quality living. The symmetry of these two are absolutely necessary. All work and no play or all play and no work can be self-defeating. However, blending labor with fun and leisure is a target worth the aim and the shooting. And there's no sweeter place than the bull's-eye of a balanced life. Yet today, few people come close to the center. Some work too much and have little or no fun while others become engrossed in entertainment, recreation and over indulgence.

Oh, go ahead and have fun, only don't let fun have the best of you. Some folks try so hard to enjoy themselves until they defeat the reason for it in the first place–to refresh, rest and replenish from work and routine. Having fun with focus should be the goal. Vacations, family reunions, hiking, biking, and trips to amusement parks and beaches are fun activities but should be balanced with allotted times for quietness and stillness. So much is going on until it's go, go, go. The "merry-go-round" of life is exciting for a while but eventually all riders want to stop and get off. Twenty-four hours in circles is not going to get it when it comes to enjoying a fulfilling life.

To get a new lease on life for returning to work more rejuvenated than ever, be wise in how you have fun. If fun is finished with a hangover, tired baggy eyes, more stress or a feeling of guilt for some ungodly thing that was done, what's the purpose? Well, there is no purpose in wasted time and energy, even in the name of fun.

> **Work and recreation should create a healthy equilibrium that enhances the quality of life.**

On the other end of the spectrum, being a workaholic can be unhealthy as well. Is it really worth it to work one's life away and miss out on all other important aspects of living, like enjoying a mate, children, family, friends, church and community? Obsessed with the next task, a labor extremist can get so caught up in their work, career or ministry that it's too late when they realize they are out of touch with their loved ones. It's a rude awakening to wake up one day and realize they don't know their wife, husband, children, family or friends anymore. So, all work and no play or recess can be just as damaging as unbalanced fun.

Many people have been caught up in a loop between work and play only to find themselves burnt out, empty and unfulfilled. For instance, rest, exercise, and healthy eating and thinking contribute to one's health and wellness. Without such basic discipline, eventually an individual will be too unhealthy to carry out his or her mission in life.

Understandably, preparation and process for success requires sacrifice. Sometimes family members must give up some of their time with loved ones who are completing a degree or special training for a specific occupation, profession, or ministry. Yet, in all the prerequisites of achievement, one should strive for balance by scheduling in family and recreational activities. Although such priorities should be automatic or "a given" and seem elementary, they are the cause of many divorces and broken relationships.

So, when is work and play balanced and effective? When they both enhance one's own life and the lives of others in some small or great way.

Work and recreation should create a healthy equilibrium that enhances the quality of life. Remember, success without good relationships and work without play can leave one empty and unfulfilled. There is no need to live under par when balance and prosperity is available to us.

> *"There is nothing better for a man, than that he should*
> *eat and drink, and that he should enjoy good in his labour.*
> *This also I saw, that it was from the hand of God."*
> - Ecclesiastes 2:24 KJV

Seizing Relaxation

"Relax, God is in charge." This simple advice pierced my mind and spirit as I read it on a small, knitted sign. Yet, as true as these words are, can we muster up enough faith to really relax? At the time I read this message, obligations and deadlines stared me in the face, subtly suggesting, "You must get things done or else."

As a publisher, I have to continuously increase my faith as I work. This means living on the cutting edge of total triumph and threatening defeat. Like Nehemiah, when he had the awesome task of rebuilding the wall around Jerusalem while enemies plotted against him, we who are called to build businesses, ministries, and other visions must do so strategically. "Those who built on the wall, and those who carried burdens, loaded themselves so that with one hand they worked at construction and with the other they held a weapon" (Nehemiah 4:17). In other words, just working without a strategy or a plan (weapons) leaves one vulnerable to the hostile elements of technological change, as well as to mental and spiritual assault. However, although the forces of intimidation are out there, the power of God is within us.

It is this inner power and strength that we must draw upon in order to complete missions and fulfill purpose. Yes, we can access the omniscient, omnipotent and infinite power of God through prayer, studying scriptures, fasting, affirmations and works of faith. Quietude and stillness are necessary to do any of the above, which explains why so many people are defused today. Too often, stress, anxiety, weariness, fear, doubt, and a host of other depleting emotions invade the soul, disrupting peace and creating chaos.

Relax, God is in charge.

All this happens due to little or no prayer and quiet time. People are just too busy for their own good.

So, now let's just stop and take a deep breath … hold it, and exhale. Here is where the ability to relax begins. The breath of life is what brought our faculties together and keeps them together. Slow, deep breathing is calming, and releases stress and tension. Once a degree of calmness is attained, the mind and energy can be effectively focused. Parents, teachers, and others who guide and mold the lives of children know how critical it is to channel their energy. Likewise, it is equally important for adults to channel theirs, which is a self-help project for them.

"For thus says the Lord God … 'In returning and rest you shall be saved; in quietness and confidence shall be your strength.'"
- Isaiah 30:15 NKJV

Section 5

ADVANCEMENT

Minding Your Business

Chapter 10

WHERE THE RUBBER MEETS THE ROAD

After all is said and done, business still has to be handled. This last chapter covers enterprising beyond the bottom line to life itself and the mandatory transactions linked to it. Business, negotiations and investments in relation to our lives are expounded on.

The Business of Life

Life means business. From the first inhale to the last exhale, some type of business transaction is made in account for human life. The birth certificate, hospital expenses, food, clothing and shelter, college tuition, earned income, taxes, funeral expenses, will and estate settlements, and so on, are basic life and death business transactions in which someone or some entity makes money. But what happens in between is a golden opportunity that should be maximized and not wasted.

Free enterprise offers vast opportunities and grand possibilities. Communist regimes have been dismantled to make room for free enterprise. Millions of people flock to the United States from around the globe to take advantage of this abundant enterprise system. They know that here, anything is possible. Yet, many citizens born within America's borders suffer from blurred vision, being so close to the forest that they cannot see the trees. Lost in the wilderness of fear, doubt, and dreamlessness, millions of Americans live in, or are on the border of poverty. They are holding on to jobs that destroy their dreams, hoping for jobs that do not exist, and praying to win the lottery. So what is the answer to this dilemma?

> **Achievements do not come without work and tests.**

God has given us the solution–Kingdom-based, free enterprise. And it is already happening! Businesses are bursting forth like never before. Some of these enterprises are first-generation businesses sustained through relentless faith and hard work. These companies, many of which are rejected by "majority" controlled financial institutions, are still moving on. "The stone which the builders rejected is the chief cornerstone" (Matthew 21:42). A Higher Power is at work, raising the least likely to succeed to a pinnacle of miraculous accomplishments.

Achievements do not come without work and tests. "When I would do good, evil is present with me" (Romans 7:21). As a visionary pursues the vision, sacrifices will have to be made to grow the new enterprise, organization, career, or ministry. The demands will require planning and working that plan. Still, all is not fair. Perseverance must become a way of life.

"For a dream cometh through a multitude of business..."
- Ecclesiastes 5:3 KJV

Leveling the Playing Field, Really?

The status quo forces have maneuvered the free enterprise system in America (and the world) to exclude many from the mainstream of big business. The discrimination has been so blatant that set-aside laws have been enacted to provide opportunity to "minority" businesspersons formerly excluded, especially in some industries.

Minority Business Enterprises (MBEs) is a term used to categorize businesses owned by people of color. Supposedly, MBEs are to be helped through special MBE programs, due to centuries of racism and denial of equal access to business development opportunities. So, the set-aside law in essence says that MBEs have a right to 15 percent of the contracts provided by public entities. But this is questionable.

Public records show that most contracts secured through MBE certification are not substantial when compared to those secured by majority-owned businesses. Certain populations are still kept out of particular industries, which hinders the economic progress of U.S. cities and states.

There is plenty of money but an excess of greed. The mismanagement of time, funds, faith, work, creativity, determination, and other God-given gifts cause what appears to be shortages. When used wisely with integrity, these resources yield money and other forms of prosperity.

Business will go on, but thank God, not as usual. We are in a new era. The old is being ushered out and the new is on the rise. Young, growing businesses must and will be developed. Owners of growing businesses must move with determination and expediency, for they are the backbone of our future economy.

Negotiation and Knowing What's Non-Negotiable

As I relaxed on a flight to Atlanta, I was impacted by a message I read in an advertisement in the airline's publication. The words read, "You don't get what you deserve. You get what you negotiate." As I thought on this message, the apparent truth within it touched me. As a business owner, I knew the power of negotiation; however, in the context of the combination of these two sentences, fresh thoughts on the subject emerged.

Negotiation is a key factor in successfully getting what we need and desire. In fact, meaningful business relationships require an introduction, a proposal, and a method of negotiation developed through faith, trust, and follow-up. On the other hand, personal relationships prosper on a "give and take," "ask and receive," "work-it-out" basis, which involves more casual negotiations. A sound objective or purpose presented with the power of persuasiveness, coupled with good communications, and backed by the substance of integrity get results.

> **You don't get what you deserve. You get what you negotiate.**

Negotiators should come to the table with respect for one another. Lack of mutual respect hinders all negotiations. Therefore, there can be no mediation or grounds for agreement. A rapport needs to be developed so that clarity and understanding can be established. Effective communications make all the difference.

Business negotiations require that each party convene, bringing something of value to exchange. Each negotiator should know the value of what he or she possesses and be able to articulate that worth accurately. Knowing in advance how much of it they are willing to give in exchange for what they will receive is key.

In life, we encounter points where we can't have it all. Our way or no way is not the way. It is at these crucial times of decision that we can choose to be flexible or rigid and stubborn. Opting to be flexible, to let go of some of what you want to accommodate some of what someone else wants can improve that relationship. And what's really happening when we opt to be flexible is negotiation. We let go, give some and receive some. Then, life can be so much nicer and more peaceful, especially in a marriage, with a co-worker or friend.

On the other hand, realize that some things and principles should not be negotiated. Truth and integrity are not negotiable. Covenant relationships are not negotiable; these include our relationship with God and relationships within the institutions of marriage and family, as well as extended family and true friendships.

No amount of money or any type of deal should ever require the breaking or betrayal of a sacred, covenant relationship. If so, walk away. There is nothing to discuss. Know when to draw the line. In fact, if a negotiator or anyone asks you to do wrong to anyone, say "no" and tell them why. If doing right destroys the deal, then so be it. Lying, cheating, and stealing is not an option.

> *"Can two walk together,*
> *unless they agree?"*
> - Amos 3:3 NKJV

Giving: The Wisest Investment

Begin all of your giving and investments as the Greatest Giver and Investor. Giving is the nature of God. Consider that our initial investment has been made by our Maker. The Giver of each breath generously bestows this vital gift that sustains us to realize our purpose or reason for living. Also, God has lavished us with many other gifts and talents that we're responsible for discovering, using and investing.

What we sow into our lives and the lives of others directly affects our level of prosperity. Being prosperous includes: wholesome relationships, personal fulfillment, a peaceful state of mind and spirit, a healthy body, and more than enough income. However, true prosperity, which involves abundance with balance in all facets of life, can easily be crowded out in our modern lifestyles.

Investing quality time with God, self, and family must be first priority. Then, one's pursued goals can manifest in an orderly manner. Prioritizing and looking at what really matters are mechanisms for staying on track. More than ever, life is filled with "stuff" that robs us of valuable time, depletes energy, and adds stress.

Getting a return on your investments is a wholesome desire. Gaining in life requires steadfast faith, persistent effort, and focus. It is imperative that one keeps his or her eyes on the prize, goal, vision, and purpose. This means that amidst distractions, challenges and setbacks, a commitment to work toward desired results or a dream must remain a priority.

> **Gaining in life requires steadfast faith, persistent effort, and focus.**

Wise investors usually gain because they know there are no short cuts to building wealth. They don't sell out honesty and integrity for a buck, nor do they selfishly hoard their wealth and knowledge. They don't neglect their spiritual, personal, and family needs.

Recently, I read about a very successful person who, at the height of his career, was faced with a serious health problem. He had already taken on a demanding major project that required a tremendous amount of his time and energy. Confronted by the stressful situation, he had to make a decision. Well, his true greatness within came forth as he stated that he would withdraw from that project to spend more time taking care of himself and his family. This is the kind of wise decision-making and proper prioritizing it takes to be a wise investor, a real winner. Sometimes we must rest and recuperate before taking on a task in order to be more focused and effective.

As we press toward our goals and desires, frequent reality checks should be made to examine not only what we are doing, but why. If our schedules allow no personal or family time, or time for other important relationships, some priorities should be rearranged. After all, what can we do with "success" if there's no one with whom to share it? The fact is, we need each other regardless of our differences. Otherwise, God wouldn't have created so many unique people on this planet.

"Cast your bread upon the waters, for you will find it after many days."
- Luke 12:29, 31 NKJV

Conclusion: Onward Resolution

Purposeful living is really a relational experience determined by how we choose to relate with ourselves, God, and others. Each of the five parts in this book–You, Others, Change, Stability, and Advancement–reveals some of the dynamics of living purposefully. Purposeful living is focusing attention and effort on what matters most according to God's word and will for your life.

It all begins with love. Nothing truly meaningful is possible without love. Love is given from God, empowering us to love ourselves and one another. From this premise the precious blessings of faith, purpose, and vision enable us to be and make a difference in this world.

Let's determine to press through, go around, and overcome the obstacles put in our way. In doing so, not only do we reap benefits but others glean as well. The benefits can be both obvious and unseen. Remember to count your blessings, which magnifies the good and brings even more blessings out of what appears to be bad or adverse situations.

Intentionally making right choices, even when it is challenging and unpopular, has been an underlying message throughout the previous chapters. Living purposefully is sometimes more thorny than rosy but yields a satisfaction from having chosen the higher road; the way of meaningful living. Dreams do come true on the high road because what manifests is God's purpose for us and not just our purpose for ourselves.

Fortunately, there are great rewards for flowing with God's plan, instead of forcing our own plans. Peace of mind and a clear conscience, provision, courage, and confidence are acquired in the process, which makes it all worthwhile. Then, after doing the tough work, take time to enjoy the fruit of your labor. It's all a part of purposeful living.

Too Much You for Yourself
or 'You Just Too Much!'

By Ella Coleman

There is too much you
for yourself
Can't be contained
up, down, right or left

There is a you overflow
to package and channel
So you are presented
with your unique mantle

Who you are
is so much to discover
Ninety percent
is still undercover

There's too much of you
the world really needs
When you hold back
many others won't succeed

From all indications
you are full to the brim
No need to spill over
Pour into her or him

A shout of praise
goes up to our God
For the abundant endowments
given you to impart

So give of you
there will be plenty left
Because there's just too much
of you for yourself

Other Books by Ella Coleman

Youth Arise! A Poetic Call to Empowerment ($14.95, paperback, ISBN# 978-0-9848025-5-5), is a clarion appeal to higher thinking and wiser living. With wisdom, guidance, rhyme and rhythm, author Ella Coleman provides a creative presentation of everything from identity, texting, social media and music, to fashions and trends, to sexuality, bullying and violence. A full gamut of the interests, issues, concerns, activities, habits and culture impacting young people today are colorfully captured in this book. It is thought-provoking, serious and fun poetry. Besides real life poetry, inclusive in this book are useful tools for building up, preserving and preparing young readers for success. "Youth Empowerment Affirmations" (YEA) encourage youth to speak constructive words.

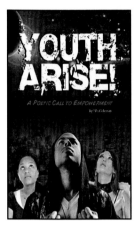

Many vital facets of life are addressed in *Poetic Overflow* ($11.95, paperback, ISBN# 978-0-9848025-4-8). Identity, attitude, creativity, faith, and the acknowledgement and expression of all types of love emerge from these poems. It has been written to personify what really matters—God and His miraculous creation, especially people and their well-being. In the midst of a world with too much destruction, *Poetic Overflow* has the ingredients to awaken readers to the beauty that is still here to enjoy within and all around us. From the inner issues of the heart, to lighthearted and fun ex-

pressions, to the aesthetic beauty of nature, this book is an adventure. Readers who pick up this book are likely to delightfully indulge in the word feast on each page.

To order books, to schedule Ella for dynamic speaking, recitations, and reading excerpts, or for a book signing event, visit EllaColeman.net; email ellavatingu@live.com.